— *Let's Win!* —

Let Wall Street Work for You

Scott Lask

Brick Tower Press
Habent Sua Fata Libelli

Manhanset House
Shelter Island Hts., New York 11965-0342

bricktower@aol.com • www.BrickTowerPress.com

Library of Congress Cataloging-in-Publication Data
Lask, Scott M.
Let's Win—Let Wall Street Work For You
p. cm.

1. Business & Economics / Investments & Securities / Analysis & Trading Strategies. 2. Business & Economics / Personal Finance / Investing. 3. Business & Economics / Finance / Wealth Management. Non-Fiction, I. Title.
ISBN: 978-1-955036-47-4, Trade Paper

July 2023

— *Let's Win!* —

Let Wall Street Work for You

Scott Lask

Acknowledgments

First and foremost, I want to thank you for buying this book. My goal was to share with you what I have learned and used to help my clients achieve their financial goals, but most importantly to write it simple English. As the famous retailer Sy Syms used to say:

An educated consumer is our best client!

My hope is this book will leave you more informed and confident in your investing.

I want to thank my wife Caren for her unconditional love and support. Marrying Caren was the best decision of my life! Also, my children Josh, Ariel and Matt for their "continuing education of their Dad"!

To my publisher, Barry Cohen, who guided me in making this book a reality far beyond my original draft. Thank you, Barry!

To my marketing Guru, PJ Ewing, your vision and dedication has made a huge difference in my advisory practice getting the right message to the public.

To Ed Imparato and Steve Cook for their trust in me and their terrific critiques helping me to craft the message. Your friendship and support mean the world to me.

To Dr. Bob Goldman and Steven Schussler, two high school friends who have changed the world and continue to inspire me. Thank you!

To John T. Colby Jr. from Brick Tower Press for all your hard work in getting the book onto the market.

Thanks to Nancy Delain for her diligence in copyrighting my book. I cannot stress enough how important her contribution was.

Also special thanks to Chris Lipper for his support, guidance and inspiration.

Last, but not least, to my colleagues at Wedbush Securities for your support.

Foreword

Scott Lask writes as a true patriot, one who embraces the American Dream and wants others to live it, too. In his book, *Let's Win; Let Wall Street Work for You*, Scott offers a common-sense approach to creating wealth and securing one's own American Dream.

Much like Scott's approach to providing financial advisory services, this book is a personal and purposeful roadmap to creating wealth strategies for the everyday investor. It is a helpful, insightful guide that outlines the appropriate times to invest or as Scott puts it, "Go Shopping," to stay the course, or to go in another direction.

Scott leverages 39 years of professional experience and knowledge to speak directly to each reader on a personal level. *Let Wall Street Work for You* is filled with witty, humorous stories that will have you thinking: H*e's writing about me*.

This book conveys a refreshing perspective on lifelong investing. Whether you are a novice or a seasoned investor, this book will uncover successful investment techniques for building wealth and minimizing risk. It will also raise important questions and generate a few red alerts that will add value to your current investment strategy.

As an educated and experienced financial executive, I have read countless books and listened to dozens of speakers on this topic. Investment strategies are often reduced to theories, algorithms, and charts - the common tools of the trade; however, the combination of a clear, concise message and executable plan are a rare find. Often absent, as well, is the link between successful investing and one's personal values.

In my opinion, successful investing is not solely derived from charts, numbers, and calculations. Successful investing involves understanding all aspects of how one measures success and significance. A holistic approach to creating wealth includes maximizing returns, minimizing risk while aligning your investment strategy with your values and personal measures of success.

The work of a successful financial adviser is premised on building a trusted relationship with the client - a relationship that not only adds value to one's portfolio but also adds value to one's life. That is a fitting description of Scott's approach to his profession.
Thank you, Scott, for your professionalism and for putting pen to paper to share your knowledge and experience. I am most grateful to call you my financial adviser and even more grateful to call you, my friend.

Ed Imparato, CMA, MBA
Senior Financial Executive and Inspired Leader
2010 CFO of the Year – Private Companies - NJBIZ

Table of Contents

WEALTH IS INEVITABLE!
SIMPLE COMMON, SENSE STEPS THAT BUILD YOUR WEALTH

Introduction

By picking up this book, you have signaled that you care about your money. That you want the BEST money can buy to grow your money so you can continue to prosper and grow your wealth! I want to share with you what I have seen for over three decades that builds wealth! I want you to have more wealth! I want to show you, you can achieve that!

I wrote this book with three goals: 

1. To get people to realize that investing is a pathway to wealth, open to everyone.

2. To strip away the layers of "marketing" that make investing more esoteric and complicated than it needs to be.

3. To share a simple, common-sense approach that has served my clients and myself extremely well, that you can use right now!

Investing is not rocket science or quantum physics. With 39 years of experience as a Financial Advisor, I know that successful investment utilizes common sense. Yes, it takes research and understanding the basics of business, but common sense is a key factor in creating wealth from investment.

I believe in the magic of compound growth and how it can build real, perpetual wealth and financial security for people.

We will take a journey together and explore case studies. You may find your experiences are very similar to others and how a few simple changes can have a profound effect on your earnings growth.

You will learn that RISK is the most important four-letter word you ever learn. The word risk is used 70 times throughout this book! Managing risk is the key to long term growth and outperformance.

We will examine how "emotions" affect your investment decisions, the dynamic of Greed vs. Fear and why you must control it, thus allowing you to prosper from it.

You will be given a Risk Management checklist that will stop you from making classic rookie mistakes and put you in an advanced position to grow your money more consistently.

Finally, you will receive Five Easy Steps to follow that will put common-sense to work for you right away. You will see, in one of the case studies, how we used these Five Easy Steps to transform a new client from thinking they would never be able to grow their account, to growing their account with less risk while being able to put more money into pure savings, as well.

At the end of each chapter, you will be given key learning points and exercises to help utilize the information.

So, I want to thank you in advance, for taking this journey with me. My hope is that this book inspires you and helps you become a more successful investor. As we begin, I would like to inspire you with this:

You are entitled to your share of global economic growth now and forever!

Now go get yours!

Chapter 1 – Unlimited Opportunity: Everyone Can Play

This book is about just that …. Using your natural instinct to build your wealth!

America is still, and always will be, the golden land of opportunity. The financial markets offer easy access to investment to create wealth for you! That's right, … you!

This book will work for you whether you are a novice investor, or you are a billionaire. It will not reveal a ground-breaking algorithm to beat the market. This book will not discuss a "proprietary strategy" and it will not promote the "voodoo" of the day.

This book is about common sense. I am going to talk to you about ideas and discipline that anyone and everyone can use to create wealth, prosperity, choice, freedom, and more happiness.

My first mentor in business told me this:

> "The thing about common sense is, it ain't too common."

Boy, truer words were never spoken. For 39 years, I have seen people make so many investing mistakes, ***myself included***. When I looked back to analyze what prompted these mistakes, I saw that in many cases, a lack of common sense – real, common sense simply was not applied. Why?

Because investing and money are emotional experiences and rarely ever logical.

Want proof?

All you need to do, is look at the market/economic cycle. Here is what I mean.

- When did people fall in love with Real Estate? When it was front page news, hyping all the money people were making and it was "safe" to do.
- When did people pile into stocks? Again, when it was "safe."

The mental path goes something like this.

"Hmm, everyone is making money here. And I am not. I want my share. I have to get in before it is too late!"

"Like most things our decisions are emotional."

Does this sound like a logical, well thought out plan? NO! But such is human nature. Like most things our decisions are emotional.

Common sense will tell you that if people who have never invested before in Risk assets are crashing the gate to get in, it is probably not going to end well. Just as we have seen in every craze in history from tulips to the DOTCOM craze, and the Real Estate bubble.

Tuning out the noise, forces us to do the math; it makes us stop and think. Sure, you are still going to make choices that don't work out, but you will make less costly mistakes that won't hurt as much. And from that, you will be able to always see more clearly, think and prosper. The markets give you unlimited opportunities and everyone can play!

Key Learning Points:

- Investing and money are highly emotional. Eliminate emotions from the equation.
- Know the market "emotional" cycle. Become aware of your investment "emotions."
- Common sense turns off the noise and lets you think.

Chapter Exercise:

1. What are your investment emotions?
2. How have your emotions affected your investment decisions?
3. What common sense approach would have helped you in the past?

Chapter 2 – Follow the Herd…Right Off the Cliff

I have met and served many wealthy people who built multi-million-dollar portfolios starting with small amounts of money. Sadly, far too many people think you need a large amount of money to start investing. Nothing can be further from the truth. This is limited thinking and will keep you trapped financially.

Warren Buffet, the legendary investor, started his portfolio with only $3,000. As of this writing, he is worth $84 BILLION dollars.[1] He is the third richest man in America, and he started with $3000 dollars!

---

[1] Sourced 7/27/2020

And while yes, he is very smart, a study of his investment philosophy is oozing with common sense. Some of his basics are:

- Buy what you understand.
- Buy companies with great management and let them run the company.
- Let your money grow over long periods time.

Common Sense! Let me give you a picture of what growth looks like. Refer to the chart below.[2]

If you invested $100 in the S&P 500 at the beginning of 2007, you would have about $360.95 at the end of 2022, assuming you reinvested all dividends. This is a return on investment of 260.95%, or **8.44% per year**.

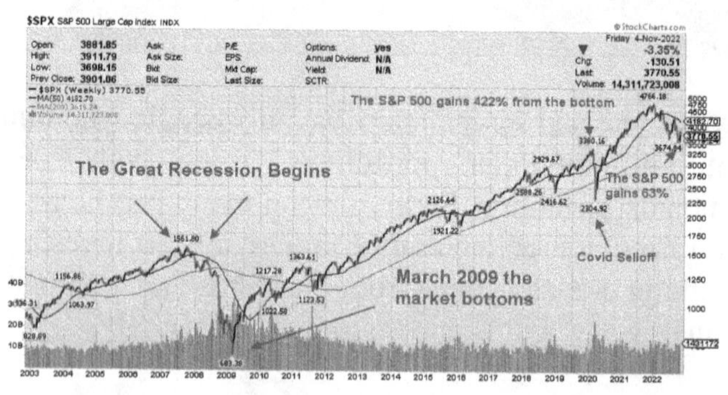

---

https://www.bing.com/search?q=forbes+400+full+list&FORM=SBRS01
2

[2] Source: StockCharts.com 7/28/2020

I clearly remember all the pundits during the height of the DOTCOM craze going on air and saying:

"Warren Buffet is yesterday's news. His style does not work anymore. He is done."

Done? While many of these "gurus" were vaporized by the crash, Buffet went onto make billions more. Common Sense! Buffet has famously advised:

"Be fearful when others are greedy and be greedy when others are fearful."

This advice is timeless.

So, I am giving you a list of common-sense rules that have worked over my career.

1. Wealth grows and expands over time.

2. Don't be a herd animal.

3. When the Uber driver is giving you "hot stock tips" be afraid.

4. When panic sets in and it is *The Walking Dead on Wall Street*, start shopping.

5. You can't own them, so own them. Buy the stock and own a piece of the company.

6. Own your slice of Global Economic growth for life.

Let's take a closer look at each of these rules.

#1 Wealth grows and expands over time. This strategy has been proven and has been financially rewarding for many. Let me give you an example I love to share with clients, friends, and prospective clients.

You are left $10,000 in 1980 with 2 conditions.

1. You must invest the money into the S&P 500 index.

2. You cannot touch the money until October 30, 2022

So, you comply and now it is October 30th[3]. OK, time to look.

Your $10,000 is now worth $997,707.35!

No matter how many ups and downs economy—and the market experienced during that period, the growth still occurs.

Are you happy?
YOU BET YOU ARE HAPPY!

---

[3] https://www.officialdata.org/us/stocks/s-p-500/1980?amount=10000&endYear=2022

So how did this happen? It is the beauty of compounding over long periods of time. As companies innovate, offer better products and services their revenues and profits grow. With more profits they can also pay out dividends. It follows that their companies (aka their stock price) are worth more money.

Albert Einstein once said "**Compound interest is the eighth wonder of the world. He who understands it, earns it; he who doesn't pays it**"[4]

So, what is this phenomenon compounding? It is growth whereby interest income, dividend income and common stock appreciation is credited to your existing investment. Here is an example I was shown early in my career.

You are given a choice: A lump sum payment of $500,000 or earning one penny that doubles every day for 30 days? Like most people I immediately said, "thank you, I will take the $500,000!"

Well, here's is what one penny earned that doubles every day for 30 days is worth?

---

[4] https://bit.ly/CompoundInterestlink

$5,368,708.50!!![5]

Pretty darn amazing!

Business owners build wealth over long periods of time. Apple® in 2000 had more cash per share on the books than their stock was selling. Apple is now worth over $1 Trillion dollars. So, if you were short term minded, you would have made money and left a fortune on the table! The list goes on:

Google®
IBM®
Amazon®
Microsoft®
Amgen®
Merck®

Long term, Large Rewards!

---

[5] https://traderlion.com/quick-reads/penny-doubled-for-30-days/

#2 Don't Be A Herd Animal!

How many times have you heard it said:

"Don't follow the herd. The crowd is always wrong. Do the opposite of the consensus."

Sure, you've heard it. Over and over, again. Have you listened and followed this advice? If you are like most people, probably not. It's ok! Following the herd is a behavioral thing. It suggests safety, something that is emotionally important. We all want to feel safe. It also validates your decision. Everyone else is doing it, so how could I be wrong? And you don't want to miss out. "Darn, everyone else is making money with this, what am I waiting for?"

Sound familiar? Has this happened to you? I know it has happened to me before I became a financial advisor. Now that I have this discipline, I can help so many more people. Had I used common sense I would have avoided a very painful experience with my first ever stock investment. I bought stock in a company called Captain Crab's Takeaway. I was convinced they would be "the McDonald's®" of the seafood business! I had delusions of making $millions$. Instead… I lost my entire investment! Common sense would have told me do not start my investment portfolio at the "riskiest end of the pool." That was before I entered the financial advisory business. But it was a great lesson that I live every day using this to help my clients and my family.

Let me really drive this point home with a little trip into the past.

The year is 1634. tulips are all the rage in Europe. They are "the" prestige and status symbol to own, like a Rolls Royce®. People can't buy tulips fast enough! At one point, tulip prices per bulb were more expensive than a small home! And everyone, and I mean EVERYONE had to own tulips. It got so crazy the markets, actually began trading tulip futures! Can you imagine tuning into CNBC or Bloomberg News in the morning and hearing what tulip futures are trading for? This craze, mania really, lasted until 1637.

Can you guess how this tulip craze ended?

KABOOM!

Why did this happen?

"When the last buyer has bought, the sellers come out. And the pain begins!"

It comes down to this: Supply vs. Demand; or as I like to say buyers vs sellers.

You see, when the last buyer has bought there is no one left to pay the last price or higher. On Wall Street, when the last buyer has bought, the sellers come out. And the pain begins!

Fortunes were lost, people wiped out! Economic activity slowed dramatically! This is seen as the first bubble burst in modern economic history. Do you see any similarities to, let's say…The DOTCOM crash or the mortgage/real estate collapse in 2008?

DON'T BE A HERD ANIMAL!

#3 When the Uber driver is giving you "hot stock tips" BE VERY AFRAID!

(note: back in the day it was a cab driver)

Let me start by saying, the Uber driver is probably a great guy/gal. And they just might be a financial genius, in which case, pay attention and take good notes. But what I have seen in over three decades as a professional investor is, when stock tips are coming from the person driving you to the airport, its GAME OVER!

Why? Because the cab driver isn't even part of the investment eco system. Let me share a personal experience. I had time to kill before an important meeting and decided to get my shoes shined. Trust me, they needed it. The gentleman shining my shoes was telling me to load the boat on shares of NORTEL. This is August 2000. The DOTCOM craze was in full bloom. (pun intended) Not long after that NORTEL imploded and its value was cut in half in one trading day. From a peak of $124/share it collapsed to 47¢ per share! Thus, began the DOTCOM crash.

We are seeing this phenomenon currently in the guise of Bitcoin, the digital currency craze. Successful investing is not about hot tips. It is about ownership of high-quality assets and businesses.

#4 When Panic Sets In, Start Shopping!

In my many years in business, I have been exposed to so many concepts, platforms, philosophies, economic indicators, and research techniques that I cannot keep count. Many have been very reliable and, in my experience the best indicator of market/economic turns has been we humans! People being people. I call it:

The Scott Lask Behavior/Misbehavior Indicator.

It has never failed me yet. Here is how it works. Supply & Demand dictates price of any kind. Supply & Demand 101: more buyers, prices rise. More sellers, prices drop. Human behavior completely drives Supply & Demand.

So here is how the Behavior/Misbehavior indicator works.

Let's say your neighbor always buys cars that cost $30,000. One day, he/she pulls into the driveway sporting a Mercedes Benz 500 C Class fully loaded, $150,000 +. ALERT, ALERT!

Similarly, your friends who always took the least expensive beach house rental and are now buying a house on Martha's' Vineyard near the Kennedy compound for $2 million dollars! ALERT, ALERT!

People are outside their financial comfort zone. In boxing, it's called "punching above your weight." When you see this behavioral shift, you're seeing the last mad dash of buyers stampeding into things they really can't afford and really shouldn't be buying.

When the last buyer has bought, the Sellers will appear. And they come out in droves!

Think 2008 and Real Estate. What happened? The bubble burst and some people were vaporized, while most just got killed. So, when you see this shift, take heed!

But that is only half of the story. Hopefully, you've taken defensive precautions when you act on the Alerts. Moves such as trimming or selling your most speculative holdings, increasing cash, etc., allow you to be ready and able to profit from the flip side. And here it is. The bubble has burst and stocks, the economy etc., are plunging. To put some color to it, everyone is running around with their hair on fire desperately selling all their stocks. It's The Walking Dead on Wall Street and Main Street. The world is coming to an end!

"Stocks are plunging… This is when you pull out your wallet and start shopping!"

This is when you pull out your wallet and start shopping! At this point you're thinking:

"OK, Scott up to now you've been making sense. But stock prices are plunging, and you want me to go shopping?"

YES!

Because, throughout history markets and economies come back. You buy when assets are cheap.

Let me put it this way. For those who know me personally, know I love French Cuff shirts! Love 'em! When my shirt maker tells me, they are having a 40% off sale, my credit card is out in a nano-second! It is bargain time. When the stock market throws a big sale (aka the market has plunged) nobody comes! Well, almost nobody. Now I want you to re-read this to really remember the Boom period when asset prices just go up, up and up, never seeming to stop rising followed by the Bust period when prices fall like a brick off the Empire State Building. You will start to remember many instances of this human behavior that truly were tell-tale signs that a shift was coming. This goes hand in hand with *"don't be a herd animal"* and if you stay alert you can profit by it.

As a learning exercise, go on the internet and look up stock prices of your favorite companies in 2008. Now see what they are selling for. Here is a very easy site to use.
https://www.marketwatch.com/tools/quotes/historical.asp

Here is a short illustrative list:[6]

Cisco Systems: $16.30 – 44.39
Johnson & Johnson: $59.83 - $133.15
IBM: 84.16 - $156.20
Apple - $12.19 - $171.95
Ford Motor: $2.29 - $10.61
Caterpillar: $44.67 - $156.49

---

[6] Source: https://www.marketwatch.com/tools/quotes/historical.asp 12/31/2008 to closing prices as of 2/16/2018

When everyone is in a panic, start shopping. You will never pick a bottom and you will be early, but as a long-term investor history has shown you will do well. Why? Because either the economy comes back, or we will all be in a foxhole.

#5 You can't own them, so *own* them!

It would be awesome if I had enough money to own Apple Corp 100%. Since I don't have a spare $1 Trillion dollars lying around, I will do the next best thing and own Apple. I will own a piece of the company. And this goes with one of my core investment values:

"I want to own a share in the global economy. And I want to own that for life!"

As we discussed in the last chapter, money invested over long periods of time really grows. Like, "fortune type" of growth. I believe in the global economy. Humans are constantly evolving. We are always innovating, making things that are faster, better, and less expensive. Being financially invested in this is a viable path to prosperity. Let's look at history. When Neil Armstrong walked on the moon in 1969 state-of-the-art computers literally filled entire rooms.

We have all read the reports that the computing power of our smart phones is bigger than the computers used to land a man on the moon!

Now this was state-of-the-art! High speed, super-duper computing. What filled a room now sits in the palm of your hand! How much wealth do think was created with these innovations? Well, Apple in their Q3 2020 earnings release showed that iPhone sale were $26.42 BILLION DOLLARS! And that is just one product from one company!

My point is, investing for the long term to grow with the global economy is a viable and logical path for financial growth. Think of what you would have missed being short term minded.

1973 – Ethernet & Internet
1976 – Personal Computer
1977 – PC Modem developed
1983 – Mobile phones
1991 – World Wide Web
1991 – e-Mail
1999 – Bluetooth

And we haven't even gotten to iPod, iPad, iPhone, the cloud, Facebook®, Twitter®, MRIs, Electric cars, and Kindle, just to name a few. All these innovations changed the world, made our lives better and yes, created large amounts of wealth!

So, I ask you,

Do you think humans are finished inventing new things?

If you answered NO, my next question is: Do you want your share of the wealth this will create? If you answered YES, then invest and invest for the long term.

Now I know some of you are going to remind me how long it took tech stocks to recover and my answer is: yes, they did and that is why you were diversified across several industries. Remember the old saying:

"As one door closes, another opens."

Don't get me wrong, you would have taken some hits during any market correction. A robust and dynamic Risk Management protocol would have helped you get through the downdraft more successfully and take advantage of new opportunities. We will discuss Risk Management in depth in Chapter 5.

The stock market reflects all trends in our economy. As technology creates new innovations companies creating change grow and replace companies with obsolete products. As an example, here is a list of the original 30 companies that made up The Dow Jones Industrial Average in 1928.

- Allied Chemical
- American Can
- American Smelting
- American Sugar
- American Tobacco
- Atlantic Refining

- Bethlehem Steel
- Chrysler
- General Electric
- General Motors Corporation
- General Railway Signal
- Goodrich
- International Harvester
- International Nickel
- Mack Truck
- Nash Motors
- North American
- Paramount Publix
- Postum Incorporated
- Radio Corporation
- Sears Roebuck & Company
- Standard Oil (N.J.)
- Texas Company
- Texas Gulf Sulphur
- Union Carbide
- U.S. Steel
- Victor Talking Machine
- Westinghouse Electric
- Woolworth
- Wright Aeronautical

Here are the 30 companies in the index today.

3M, American Express, Amgen, Apple, Boeing, Caterpillar, Chevron, Cisco Systems, Coca-Cola, Disney, Dow, Goldman Sachs, Home Depot, Honeywell, IBM, Intel, Johnson & Johnson, JP Morgan Chase, McDonald's, Merck, Microsoft, Nike,

Procter & Gamble, Salesforce, Travelers, UnitedHealth, Visa, Walgreens, and Walmart.

Not one company from the 1928 list is in the index today. Many have gone out of business, while others have been bought by other companies. The question is:

What caused the changes?

The simple answer is people invented a better mouse trap. Technology! The Victor Talking Machine Company made essentially the first phonographs. For those born during the 1990s or later, this was a record player used to listen to music. Today we listen to music on our phones, our iPad, our computers and occasionally our car radio. And that is the reason why The Victor Talking Machine Company was replaced by Apple!

Key Learning Points:

1. Wealth grows and expands over time. Give your money a chance to compound!
2. Don't be a herd animal.
3. When the Uber driver is giving you "hot stock tips" be afraid.
4. When panic sets in and it is The Walking Dead on Wall Street, start shopping.
5. You can't own them, so own them.
6. Own your slice of Global Economic growth for life.

Chapter Exercises:

1. What valuable lesson did you learn from The Tulip Craze?
2. How would you avoid investing like a Herd Animal?
3. Why should you fear when others are greedy?

Chapter 3 - It Really is Simple, Silly!

The challenge with learning about anything outside your own skill set is, so many people make things complicated. They don't mean to, but they do without realizing it. Let me give you an example.

Have you bought a software program that was heralded as "plug 'n play," only to find:

1. It is not plug 'n play.

2. You do not understand the prompts.

3. When you call the company's support line they speak to you in "code," only to find out you are missing a driver. Why didn't they tell you that when you bought their software?

It's frustrating and maddening, right? Now in all fairness to tech support people, they really do know their stuff. I would be stuck without them. But, they speak a different language --- one I don't understand; no matter how hard I try!

Every now and again I connect with a tech support person that talks to me in simple, direct language and my problem is fixed in minutes. And I take their direct line down because if I need help again, they will keep it simple and fast.

Well, it is the same in investments. Human nature --- we want to sound smart and knowledgeable. We believe (falsely) that big fancy, technical terms will impress people and motivate them to employ our expertise to manage their money. NOT!

In my profession, I can tell you people do not care when you "jargon up." Consider the two descriptions below, theoretically explaining the same investment.

"This is a low Beta, High Alpha portfolio with a high coefficient of parity to the benchmark, S&P 500 matched by strong correlative properties."

or,

"This fund doesn't have the big swings that other funds have and has good growth potential and tracks the S&P 500 closely."

How would you prefer someone talk to you about this investment?

In fact, even the most sophisticated investors will tell you they appreciate simple, direct explanations of investment features and benefits.

So, when you educate yourself about analytical tools for investing, keep it simple. Some basic guidelines to look for:

- **Strong balance sheets** – the company has more assets than liabilities. This is especially important when the economy slows or goes into a recession. Some examples would be comparing Sears Roebuck to Apple. Sears had a crushing debt load that forced the company to shutter stores, lay off employees, causing the stock to plunge from $126/share in 2007 to 10₵/share currently! Compare that to Apple that has over $48 billion in cash with the stock going from $5.75/share to $153/share.

- **Cash on the books** – just like your own finances a strong cash reserve lets you meet day to day needs. It is a cushion against the lean times, and it also offers access to cash to take advantage of opportunities.

- **Good debt management** – simple example; the company has $2 cash to cover $1in debt vs. the company has $1 in cash to cover $2 debt. Which company would you rather run?

- **Rising dividend history** - Dividends are payments a company makes to share profits with its stockholders. Companies that raise dividends are growing.

- **How essential is their product(s)** – Is the company's products a basic necessity or a passing fad? Is it Johnson & Johnson providing health care and pharmaceuticals for our health or a Peloton where you can exercise anywhere with no equipment or join a gym?

- **How much competition is there?** – Competition is the mother of innovation. Is the company capable of growing its customer base or will innovation set them back--or worse, make their products irrelevant? Think vinyl albums being rendered obsolete with the advent of cassette tapes or CDs.

Here is another example of keeping it simple. Look at what companies you do business with already. What is in your driveway, your den, your kitchen? One of the best investments I ever made came from my wife.

We were young parents of a 2-year-old and a 4-year-old. They needed shoes. My wife Caren tells the salesclerk she only wants to see Stride Rite shoes. The salesclerk wants to show other brands as well and Caren is having none of it. She proceeds to *"educate"* this man that Stride Rite shoes are the only shoes she will let our children wear and launches into a feature and benefits presentation so enthusiastic, you would have thought she was the CEO of the company!

Well $175 later, (this is 1989) we leave the story with happy, well shod kids. That night I pull together all the research on Stride Rite and discover a great company! I bought shares at $14,16, & 19. Two years later shares of Stride Rite changed hands at $42 per share.

So, what are you buying? Who are you giving your money to? Look around your home. What is hot with high schoolers? What companies do your doctor and pharmacist prefer to work with? Watch for trends. Microsoft grew so big and their stock made investors so much money the term: MICROSOFT MILLIONAIRES became common, everyday language.

COMMON SENSE!

Key Learning Points:

- Don't make things complicated. Keep it simple.
- Educate yourself on investment basics.
- Analyze stocks as if you were going to buy the business.
- Companies that you buy products from may be a good starting point to identify potential investments.

Chapter Exercises:

1. Make a list of products you own in your home, etc.
2. Determine how many of these companies are publicly traded.
3. Match this list against your investments. How many do you own?
4. Look at the ten-year performance of the names on your list.

Chapter 4- Risk, T.O.R.© & Risk Management

RISK is the most important four-letter word you will ever learn. Learn it well, if you want to be a successful investor. Webster's dictionary defines risk as:

1: possibility of loss or injury: peril

2: someone or something that creates or suggests a hazard

3a : the chance of loss or the perils to the subject matter of an insurance contract; *also* : the degree of probability of such loss

b : a person or thing that is a specified hazard to an insurer

c : an insurance hazard from a specified cause or source

- war *risk*

4: the chance that an investment (such as a stock or commodity) will lose value.

For our purposes, numbers 1 and 4 are representative of risk to money. Risk is an "intellectual concept" for many *UNTIL*...

You lose money!

I have seen it play out. It goes something like this:

You invested $1 Million dollars into a growth portfolio. And for the first several years it really did grow! In fact, it has grown to $1.7 Million! All is right with the world. Life is great, and the gravy is flowing!

Then… in what feels like the blink of an eye…the economy goes south, the market craters and your $1.7 Million is now worth $800,000! (MOMMA!!!)

"What happened? Where'd my money go?"

You, friend, have just experienced RISK. Welcome to the RISK ZONE!

OK. Breathe! It is going to be OK. Now let's be clear, all investments carry risk. Risk is inescapable. To be successful as an investor, you have to, in my opinion, focus more on the risk levels you are taking than the expected rate of growth projected by your advisor.

Every 21st century advisor has analytic tools available to project expected risk, yet many prospective clients I work with have no idea how much risk they are taking. I believe many advisors do not talk about risk completely for two reasons:

1. They aren't utilizing these analytics or do not have access to them.

2. They are reluctant to emphasize risk and risk management for fear of scaring off prospective clients.

To be clear, I am emphasizing that Risk Analytics just like Growth Analytics, are only forecasts. These are nothing more than guidelines. If we could put exact numbers out there everyone would live in the Caribbean and own 100-foot yachts.

But these tools are critical to designing your portfolio, which I refer to as:

Your Future & Happiness!

What I have found to be a prudent policy is this. You want a "reasonable rate of return" at a level of risk that will let you succeed as a long-term investor. In simple terms, ***you must be paid for the risk you are taking!***

If you're not being properly compensated for the risk you take, why bother? Let's look at it another way.

You are interviewing prospective new advisors and have narrowed down your search to two professionals. Both advisors have determined you are best served with a Balanced Model allocation. Both models have an expected average annual rate of return of 6.2% for the next twenty years. However, both advisors have a different projection for your risk. Advisor A projects you will lose 13% in a bad year. Advisor B projects you will lose you 10% in a bad year. Which advisor are you going to hire? Advisor B obviously!

Now let's look at the Sequence of Returns in table 5.1.

The sequence of returns can have a dramatic impact on your retirement

Withdrawals at the wrong time can cause a retirement portfolio to run out of money.

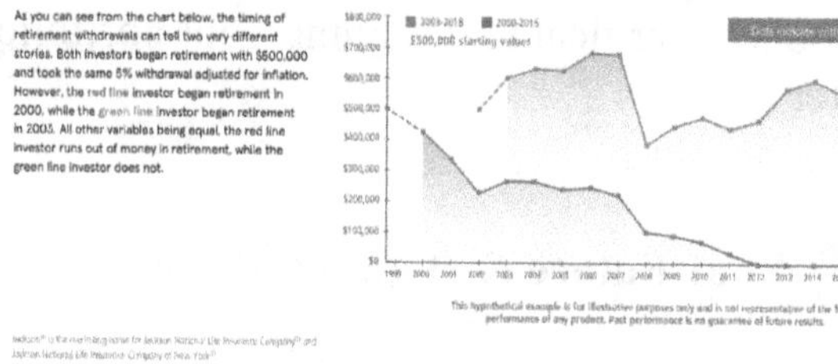

This table assumes the following:

- You are withdrawing 5% annually from your account.
- Account A started withdrawals in an "up" market while account B started withdrawals in a "down" market.

ARE YOU BEING PAID FOR THE RISK YOU ARE TAKING?

Account A is still going strong after 25 years. However, Account B runs out of money in only 13 years. Believe me, this is a very real possibility for too many people. Therefore, managing your risk is paramount to making your money last!

If you're not sure, don't know and want to know where you stand, have that conversation with your advisor now!

The other thing that is critical to find out is:

Are you emotionally in sync with your portfolio's risk exposure? Let me explain what I mean.

Let's say your $1,000,000 portfolio is designed so that in a down year your expected loss will be approximately 12%!

So, your intellectual mind says 12% is reasonable since I have been growing nicely. I can handle that.

Your emotional mind however says, "Whoa! That is a loss of $120,000!!!"

A completely different dynamic. So, it is critically important that your personal Risk level is aligned with your portfolio's. The benefits are:

- No panic attacks.
- No being blindsided.
- Avoiding having to make emotionally charged decisions which are usually very bad for you.

OK, so now you know you must be able to quantify your risk and you need to be paid for the risk you take. You need a Risk Management Plan. This topic is so huge, that I will have to write a book solely devoted to it. But for our purposes today, let's look at a MUST HAVE LIST of 5 things. for your risk management program.

1. Know your risk.

2. Know your daily cash liquidity needs.

3. Have an advisor who can demonstrate a comprehensive Risk Management program and be able to scale it.

4. Transfer risk wherever possible.

5. You must work with an advisor who has analytics to measure risk and identify changes in risk levels.

Let's discuss each in more detail.

#1 Know Your Risk

We have already illustrated why this is so critical as shown in tables 5.1 and 5.2. I simply want to reinforce the concept.

The less you lose the faster you will recover!

#2 Know Your Daily Cash Liquidity Needs.

Financially speaking, is there any worse feeling then when you don't have money? You need a new roof, your car died, there is a huge business opportunity and you don't have the money! You feel just awful! This is why you must have ready cash. Now I know, with high earners, sometimes it seems impossible to save. The good news is it is a simple fix. All you need to do is set up automatic deposit into a savings account that meets two criteria:

1. The account does not have checks or a debit card.

2. The bank must be "inconvenient" to get to. Your money needs be hard to get to.

3. Set up an ACH for a set amount of money every paycheck. ACH is fancy language for an automatic deduction from your paycheck from your payroll department direct to your savings.

If you follow this simple strategy, you will build cash reserves that grow and will be there when you need it. And one of the greatest benefits for you, is emotional. What do I mean? You will eliminate an enormous amount of stress from your life. You will avoid punishing negative feelings that hurt you and hold you back. You will go from a *"how am I going to handle this?"* mindset to *"no problem, I've got this. No sweat!"*

You will sleep better. There will be harmony in the house. You can maintain your long-term investment portfolio without interrupting your plan. Life will be better and more fun.

#3 Have an advisor who can demonstrate a comprehensive Risk Management program and be able to scale it.

Clearly it makes sense that you work with a Financial Advisor who can demonstrate a comprehensive Risk Management strategy. It is your money at risk, so don't you deserve the best Risk Management tools available?

I know from day to day experience many investors desperately need more information and guidance about Risk Management strategies, tools, and techniques. Here is a short list of MUST HAVE deliverables you should be receiving.

- A dynamic rebalancing plan: Rebalancing is the process of buying and selling portions of your portfolio in order to set the weight of each asset class back to its original state.

- A definable & disclosed Risk Management strategy: a customized plan to set downside loss limits as well as upside capture.

- A numerical Risk/Reward analysis: Simply put; for every dollar you may lose how many dollars can you potentially gain in profit. Typically expressed as a ratio; ie: 1:1, 2;1.

- A method to sync your portfolio risk with your emotional risk: Money decisions are highly emotional. They are driven typically by Greed or Fear. For a Financial Advisor to be effective, he or she must understand how each client sees money and how they react "emotionally" to market swings, loss, profit potential and everything between.

There are many more, but these, in my experience are absolutely essential.

#4 Transfer Risk

In our practice we apply our TOR program. It stands for Transfer of Risk. The concept is simple. We all buy life insurance. Why do we do this? To protect our families financially should we meet an early death. What you are doing is saying "I am not willing to take the financial risk for my family if I am not here to provide for them"?

So, with your premium payments you have "transferred" that risk to the insurance company. It is off your personal balance sheet. And we do this with many other areas of our lives, don't we? Auto insurance, home insurance, liability insurance, key-person insurance, etc.

Where we see huge gaps that put people like you at risk are:

- Retirement Income
- Longevity
- Long Term Care
- Health Insurance.

Too often, these areas are overlooked for various reasons. Often times, they are based on faulty assumptions. There are options to transfer some or all of these risks. Worse, people are not being educated adequately to their exposure and to their available options.

Many over the age of 50 list their chief worries as:

1. Having enough retirement income

2. Not outliving their money

3. Running out of money due to health care costs.

As I mentioned, there are options available to manage these additional risks. Furthermore, often there are special needs situations that families face. Again, you need to know how you can manage and transfer these risks.

Please, please, please discuss these topics with your advisors!

#5 Risk Analytics

All advisors and investment firms should have access to analytics to measure or quantify risk expectations. As we have discussed before, risk awareness is absolutely essential to all investment decisions, whether it is a stock, a bond, a mutual fund, real estate, or direct equity into a business venture.

A big mistake made by many is thinking that risk is static.

IT IS NOT!!!

Risk is dynamic. It changes with every tic of the economy.

In the investment world there are many ways to measure and analyze risk.

- Price earnings ratio - the current market price of a company share divided by the earnings per share of the company.

- Debt to equity ratio: how much debt the company owes versus the value of their common stock. Low ratios indicate strong financials. High numbers pose more risk.

- Price to Book Value: A comparison of total value of the company's -publicly traded stock versus the value of the security or asset as entered in the company's books.

- Yield (yes yield!): how much income an investment generates, separate from the principal. Examples are dividends and interest.

- Dividend coverage ratio: The dividend coverage ratio measures the number of times that a company can pay dividends to its shareholders.

- Price chart: a graph that shows you the price of a stock over a specific period of time.

- Standard deviation: a fancy way to identify how much price movement is normal and how much is extreme.

- Monte Carlo simulations: It is a technique used to understand the impact of risk and uncertainty.

Your Risk Number:

Do you know how much risk you are taking? I am not referring to your investor classification; conservative, growth, etc.

Do you know, approximately how many dollars your portfolio would drop by the markets sell off, go into a recession?

Let me ask you this question: Which would hurt more?

Your investments are down 15% or your investments dropped by $150,000 dollars? (aka your money)

Your Risk Number is quantitative way to pinpoint how much risk you are comfortable with & can afford! How much risk your current investments are taking in real time dollars. And how much risk you need to take to achieve your goals.

The scale is 0 to 100 with 0 meaning you take no risk and 100 you are all risk. If you are a more moderate & balanced investor your Risk number may range 45 to

55 which has the risk probability of losing 8.8% to 11.31%.[7]

But what if your current investments had a Risk number ranging 75-85? Now your risk is your down 16% to 20%!

Clearly there is a gap between what you want your money to do and what your money will do.

This one metric has been a game changer. Risk management is so critical to long-term success and utilizing every viable tool we can use to identify critical gaps and close is our mantra. There is no perfect world especially in the financial markets. But with risk management, every little bit helps.

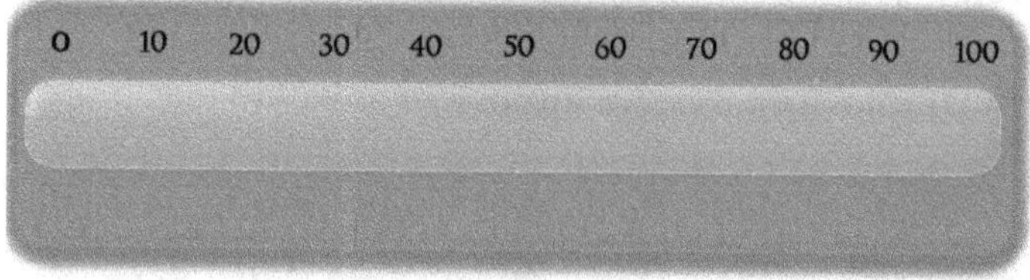

And many more! Any financial advisor can educate you on these measures.

For our purposes we will keep it simple.

[7] Source : Riskalyze Analytics.

Scott Lask rule #1 – As price rises, the more your risk rises.

Why? GRAVITY! The higher something is the further it can fall.

What fuels price rise?

More buyers than sellers. Now before you tell me not to be a wisenheimer, this is 100% true. The real question is:

Why are there more buyers than sellers and what is driving this behavior?

As an example, if the economy is turning around after a recession, companies may start earning more money, spend more on expansion adding to economic growth, wage increase, dividend increases, etc. You get the idea.

As the economy expands, don't you think it would be in your best interest to have analytic tools that measure "how much gas is left in the tank?"

To put it in more simplistic terms, let's say at the beginning of expansion your portfolio is expected to earn 6.2% on average per year and has expected risk of 10.8%. As the expansion swings into full gear, your expected rate of return drops to 5.8% but your expected risk grows to 11.8%. Now you are earning less and risking more. Wouldn't it be a good idea to at least re-evaluate and bring your risk exposure back into line? Of course, it is.

I cannot urge you enough, to keep a sharp eye on the risk you are taking! You'll thank me.

Key Learning Points:

- Transfer risk wherever possible
- Have a genuine Risk Management strategy that is flexible and sensitive to macro trends in the stock market.
- Be paid for the risk you are taking.
- Be aware of the Sequence of Returns.

Chapter Exercises:

- Have your advisor put a number on your portfolio risk. The technical term is Standard Deviation.
- Get clear on the downside $dollar amount your investments could lose in down markets. Make the math personal; it is your money.
- Review all your insurances to make sure you are transferring all the risk you can.
- Have a conversation with your advisor about how market returns may affect you when you retire.

Chapter 5 – Your Menu. A smorgasbord of pathways

Like all marketplaces, Wall Street continues to innovate solutions. From a traditional stocks and bonds only model the industry now offers many different entrees into stocks, bonds, mutual funds, Exchanged Traded Funds (ETFs), cross the board exposure to all sectors including private equity hybrids. Private placements, managed futures funds, direct access to institutional money managers, commodities, real estate investment trusts. (REITs). I am sure I have overlooked a few.

Let's unpack each of these and provide you with the highlights. But first you and I must agree on one thing.

You are responsible to learn about these pathways if you choose to invest in any of these! No ifs, ands or buts!!

I say it not only because *it is* Best Practice, but it is also the responsible thing to do. You owe it to yourself to be careful and smart with your money.

So, do we have a deal?
I know you said yes!

Common stock: is a security that represents ownership in a corporation.

Preferred stock: is a different type of equity that represents ownership of a company and the right to claim income from the company's operations.

Convertibles: is a security—usually a bond or a preferred stock—that can be converted into a different security—typically shares of the company's common stock.

Bonds: are a debt obligation, like an IOU. Investors who buy bonds are lending money to the company, a government agency or a municipality issuing the bond. Investors receive interest income typically every six months and the promise of return of their face value principal when the bond matures. Maturities span from months to as many as 30 years or more.

The positive to investing in bonds is receiving income on a scheduled basis. For retirees this can be a huge benefit to supplement their income and spending. The bond market is huge. At the end of 2021 the global bond market was valued at $119 Trillion Dollars with America accounting for $46 Trillion. Liquidity is a benefit.

The negatives for bonds are changes in interest rates. The risk that interest will rise after you invest exists. On the flip side when interest rates go down high paying bonds you own can be "called"; simply retired early because the issuer can borrow at lower cost to their entity.

Bonds can be a potent, effective, and satisfying component of your portfolio. It is a conversation worth having.

Mutual Funds: is a large investment portfolio you can buy shares in that is managed by professional money managers. It offers the benefit of buying an established, diversified portfolio with a management team. There are several different classes of funds with different fee structures.

ETFs: is a basket of securities that trades on an exchange just like a stock does. ETF share prices fluctuate all day as the ETF is bought and sold; this is different from mutual funds, which only trade once a day after the market closes. ETFs are typically pre-set portfolios versus mutual funds that buy and sell frequently.

REITs: are companies that own or finance income-producing real estate across a range of property sectors. REITs cover a broad spectrum of the real estate market ranging from residential, to apartment buildings, office complexes, warehousing to name some of the current sectors offered. They offer the potential for income and growth. They trade on major exchanges and offer daily liquidity. It is recommended you consult with your CPA regarding taxation of REITs.

Private Placements: refers to the process of raising capital that involves selling of securities to a selected group of investors. There is a limited number of qualified investors who subscribe to the offering

There are stringent financial requirements & qualifications that each investor must meet under SEC Regulation D. These investments are typically illiquid, entail a high degree of risk, long term and the investor must demonstrate the ability to absorb loss. The growth potential can be substantial, but you must understand you can lose all your money.

Managed Futures: refers to an investment where a portfolio of futures contracts is actively managed by professionals. Futures contracts are agreements to buy or sell at a set price, at a future date, commodities, equity index options, fixed income options to name a few. Managed Futures are an alternative investment category and often used to hedge other investment assets. *Potential investors are cautioned to fully educate themselves on the risks, costs, taxation as well as their financial suitability to invest in this space.*

Commodities: is a basic good used in commerce that is interchangeable with other goods of the same type. Raw materials, metals, oil, agricultural products, natural gas are examples of basic commodities that are traded on major exchanges. This is an alternative investment category that is quite used to hedge other portfolio assets.

A fixed annuity is **an insurance contract that promises to pay the buyer a specific, guaranteed interest rate on their contributions to the account**. By contrast, a variable annuity pays interest that can fluctuate based on the performance of an investment portfolio chosen by the account's owner.

Annuities: are a contract between you and an insurance company in which you make a lump-sum payment or series of payments and, in return, receive regular disbursements, beginning either immediately or at some point in the future.

The two most popular contracts are Fixed Rate Annuities and Variable Annuities. Annuities are used to provide a steady stream of income to the annuitant. They have been a useful tool in retirement planning. Today's Variable Annuity contracts may provide investors with solutions for their retirement planning. They offer flexibility of investment options and income benefits.

I want you, the reader, to understand you must carefully weigh out all the factors of how annuity contracts are structured, all the benefits, limitations, surrender periods, surrender charges and taxation to highlight some key due diligence points.

The goal of investing is to grow your wealth and create financial security. For most people, that means building for a safe and secure retirement. The key is understanding how much income you will need to keep living your lifestyle.

You should add in an inflation number and get an idea of what your potential health care costs may be. The link below is one of many retirement income calculators. It is highly recommended that you consult with all your financial professionals to craft your plan.

https://www.bankrate.com/retirement/retirement-plan-calculator/

Key Learning Points:

1. There is a wide variety of investment vehicles you can invest in.
2. Learn about the investments that can best help you and meet your specific needs, goals, and desires.
3. Research professional advisors to see what extra added value they can add to your plan and growth.
4. Don't play hit or miss. Spend the time to develop and or improve your plan.

Chapter Exercises:

1. Make a list of the different types of investments you own: common stock, mutual funds, Bonds, bond funds, CDs, Treasuries, annuities et al. If you are a new investor identify the investments that serve you best.
2. Do a comparison analysis of what types you own versus investment areas you haven't yet put money into.
3. Stress test your investments for downside risk (Standard Deviation), potential growth, current income and economic policy alignment.

Chapter 6– The Market Is on Sale!

Every one of us has things we will jump to buy when we can buy at big discounts. Clothing, appliances, technology, cars, gadgets, etc. Whatever your fancy, you hear there is going to be a big sale and you are ready to buy. Think of Black Friday. People leave Thanksgiving dinner to wait on line for hours, usually in the freezing cold, so they can buy Christmas gifts on the cheap! Folks are practically killing each other just to get into the store!

So how come, when the stock market sells off, aka *a big sale*, nobody shows up? In fact, everyone is running for the door with their hair on fire!

Why?

Investors can't get out of the market fast enough. BIG MISTAKE! Sadly, this is very common among private investors. In Wall Street terms this rush to the exit is called "capitulation." I like to call it *"Cherry picking time."* Why? Because some of the greatest companies in the world are selling for a lot less money! When you see this panic, know that historically this tends to be when prices bottom out and the trend is about to reverse back up. Need proof?

1987 – Market crashes in October. One year later the DJIA closes up 22.9%!

1989 – The LBO market collapse. The Dow dropped from 2768 in September to 2496 by October 16, 1989; a drop of 9.8%! The Dow closed the year at 2753 up from 2144 for a 28.4% gain for 1989!

1997 – The Asian contagion! Dow plunges from 8250 to 7600 in the month of August! The Dow closes 1997 at 7908 up from 6442 1/1/1997 for a gain of 22.75%!

2001-2003 – The DOTCOM crash! Dow plunges from 10,021 to 8341 during 2002. The Dow closes at 10,425 in 2003 a gain of 25% from the lows.

2008 – The world collapsed! The Dow craters from 13,264 to 8776 for the year losing 33.8%! OUCH! As of this writing the Dow Jones Industrial Average stands above 34,000!

> Scott Lask Rule #2 – When everyone is selling, GO SHOPPING!

One phenomenon I want to discuss with you is the emotional impact of market selloffs. For the record, I am not a trained psychological clinician, nor do I hold any degrees in psychology, psychotherapy, or medicine. What I am is a keen observer. So, here is how it goes.

Euphoria – the wondrous feeling as stock prices rise continuously. Life is grand, and your money just keeps growing, easy as pie. It doesn't get better than this!

The Big "UH-OH!" – Suddenly, the market is selling off. No one seems concerned. There is no news, so nothing to be concerned about. Because the market doesn't go up every day… just mostly every day! (Euphoria still at work)

But then, prices start dropping. No, not just dropping. They are plunging! Like a ball thrown off the Empire State building. Sellers are coming out of the woodwork and it is PANIC time…or as I like to say…

"It's the Walking Dead on Wall Street!"

And it gets worse, because now the media jumps in. Since bad news always sells best, they hammer away at their DOOM & GLOOM reporting. Fear is now the dominant emotion. The reptilian brain kicks into survival mode and "flight" takes precedence over "fight."

And just like that the "contraction" mind set takes over. You want to hold onto what you have left. Desperately! The driving emotions of fear and panic lead to bad decisions that have huge consequence. Let's look at an example of what goes through your mind.

"Whoa! I am losing money hand over fist. I can't afford this. I shouldn't have put so much money in the market (aka remorse). Maybe I should sell and stop the bleeding. I am scared to death and I don't want to lose it all. Somebody HELP ME!!!!

At this point, you can almost see Rod Sterling from the Twilight Zone appear in your mind's eye and he is saying:

"You're traveling through a new dimension. A dimension where your money is evaporating..."

For those of you not old enough to remember the TV show, click on YouTube and type in "The Twilight Zone" and you'll understand.

From many years of experience, I can tell you that this level of fear and anxiety can be dramatically reduced by applying:

COMMON SENSE!

Here's how you do that!

Too many people invest far more than they can afford and that almost always ends badly. This condition, which I call, "investus greedus" is the cause of investor regret. This condition can be easily corrected. Here is how: LIQUIDITY. That's right, liquidity, ample cash on hand. The reason why folks become desperately scared is they don't have enough ready cash to work with and deal with life.

> **Scott Lask Rule #3**: Invest only the amount that you can sleep at night with.

If you have $1million dollars in the market but you only have $25,000 liquid cash and the market drops 10-15%. You're going to feel anxiety. And of course, now life happens.

- Your car dies.
- Your taxes are due.
- Your boiler needs to be replaced.

Your lack of cash makes it difficult to stay fully invested. So now, because of your anxiety and several unexpected but expensive needs, you cash out of some of your portfolio. Imagine this is when the Dow Jones is above 34,000. Fast forward and the Dow is now 24,000! This happens because people do not keep enough ready cash, aka savings, available to be able to ride out the market/economic corrections as life happens.

Let's look at two scenarios.
Scenario #1- $1,000,000 invested
$25,000 in ready cash

Scenario #2 - $800.000 invested
$200,000 in ready cash

Which one lets you:

- Ride out market corrections.
- Allows you to buy stock/funds at lower prices.
- Deal with life
- Sleep at night.

While this is a simplistic example, I know you all answered Scenario #2.

The lesson here is to invest an amount you can live with, and leave invested because you have enough ready cash to be able to meet unexpected contingencies and that is how you will achieve a portfolio for life!

Remember, everyone agrees investing over the long term has produced greater wealth building success than trying to be smarter than the market. The phenomenon of compounding works brilliantly if given time to work. Again, I point you back to my original example of $10,000 invested in the S&P 500 in 1980 growing to $760,000 by December 2017! No magic. Just COMMON SENSE.

Key Learning Points:

- Learn to take advantage of market sell-offs to buy at lower prices.
- Historically, large market sell offs are followed by rallies.
- Be aware of the "emotions" of investing.

Chapter Exercises:

1. Review how your investments performed During the crash of 2008. (if you weren't invested, study the market performance. History tends to repeat itself, so you may see this material again!)
2. What would you do differently in hindsight?
3. Devise your plan for the next big sell-off.

Chapter 7 – Broker, Robo or Financial Advisor

There are multiple platforms and pathways to execute your investment plan that offer many features, benefits, conveniences and cost structures. As consumers, we should be compelled to "do our homework" to determine we are buying what we need, what we want and a solution that best serves our needs. Let's look at what is most commonly used by investors.

Broker: The dictionary defines a broker as:

a person who buys and sells goods or assets for others.

This is the platform that is ideal for the "do it yourselfer" ("DIY") investor. These are folks who have the time, have educated themselves on financial markets, in many cases have a tremendous passion for the process and have done well for themselves going it alone. Brokerage (the business or service of acting as a broker) is the most efficient platform for them to use. They truly only need a platform that allows them to buy, sell and custody their assets.

While this venue is typically to buy, sell or custody assets, some firms may offer discounted packages that include some research and advisory services.

Robo Advisor

The 21st Century experience is Technology. It is everywhere and a part of everything. As such, it is no surprise that the financial services industry has embraced it. Hence, the advent of Robo Advisor!

According to Wikipedia;

***Robo-advisors** or **Robo-advisers** are a class of financial adviser that provide financial advice or Investment management online with moderate to minimal human intervention.[1] They provide digital financial advice based on mathematical rules or algorithms. These algorithms are executed by software* *and thus financial advice does not require a human advisor. The software utilizes its algorithms to automatically allocate, manage and optimize clients' assets.*

This is also another platform for the "do it yourselfers." The emphasis here is:

- Minimal human contact
- Computer driven solutions (no human input)
- Low costs

Robo Advisors are a self-guided online wealth management service that provides automated investment advice at low costs and low account minimums, employing portfolio management algorithms. Legally, the term "financial advisor" applies to any entity giving advice about securities.

Most robo-advisor services are instead limited to providing portfolio management (i.e. allocating investments among asset classes) without addressing issues such as estate and retirement planning and cash-flow management, which are also the domain of financial planning.

Financial Advisors:

Are licensed professionals whose chief function is to:

- Listen to you

- Formulate a plan that is customized to you
- Provide multiple resources
- Educate you

Financial advisors are highly regulated and adhere to a high standard of conduct. They are compensated for their work either by commissions or a fee-based contract. One of the key benefits of working with a Financial Advisor is their ability to remain objective. I discuss more about Financial Advisors in chapter 8.

So, how do you "shop for an advisor"? Here is a list of questions to help you.

1. What is your specialty?

2. What is your overall investment philosophy?

3. How long have you been an advisor? (obvious question)

4. Why did you become an advisor?

5. Describe your team.

6. Do you have minimums?

7. Are you fee based, or commission based?

8. What is your Risk Management strategy?

9. What does your service model look like?

10. Do you personally manage my money or do you hire managers?

Key Learning Points:

- You have several options to manage your money.
- Each option has advantages depending on your preference as well as negatives.

Chapter Exercises:

- Are you a "do-it-yourselfer" or do you prefer professional advice?
- Are you getting what you need and expect from your current option?

Chapter 8 -- Types of Accounts

There are many different accounts you can utilize in your pursuit of wealth. Some are pension related. Some are to save for education. While other accounts could be utilized for estate planning, special needs, or simply to invest personal money. If you are an experienced investor, the detail below may be redundant. Feel free to skip to the next chapter. For those of you who are new to the investment world, I hope this list will be informative and helpful.

Individual Account:
An account set up in your name or jointly with other owners. Joint ownership accounts are typically either Joint Tenants with Rights of Survivorship (JTWROS) or Joint Tenants in Common (JTIC)

JTWROS is used with spouses because it transfers the assets to the survivor upon death of one of the owners. With JTIC, each tenant owns a share of the account and there are no rights of survivorship. Each tenant can stipulate in a will how they want their assets distributed at death. It is important to note that individual accounts are taxable. From a planning perspective this is important.

IRA Accounts:
This is the well-known Individual Retirement Account. IRAs are an investing tool individuals use to earn and earmark funds for retirement savings. There are several types of IRAs:

Traditional IRA:
Is an Individual Retirement Account to which you can contribute pre-tax or after-tax dollars, giving you immediate tax benefits if your contributions are tax-deductible. With a Traditional IRA, your money can grow tax-deferred, but you'll pay ordinary income tax on your withdrawals, and you must start taking distributions after age 72.

Roth IRA:
Is an Individual Retirement Account to which you contribute after-tax dollars. While there are no current-year tax benefits, your contributions and earnings can grow tax-free, and you can withdraw them tax- and penalty-free after age 59½ and once the account has been open for five years. Other advantages of having a Roth IRA include:

- **No contribution age restrictions**. You can contribute at any age as long as you have a qualifying earned income.
- **No Required Minimum Distributions (RMDs)**. There are no mandatory withdrawals, allowing your savings to continue to grow even during retirement.

- **No income taxes for inherited Roth IRAs**. If you pass your Roth IRA onto your heirs, their withdrawals will also be income tax-free.

SIMPLE IRA:
(**S**avings **I**ncentive **M**atch **Pl**an for **E**mployees) allows employees and employers to contribute to traditional IRAs set up for employees. It is ideally suited as a start-up retirement savings plan for small employers not currently sponsoring a retirement plan.

SEP IRA: is a plan that can provide a significant source of income at retirement by allowing employers to set aside money in retirement accounts for themselves and their employees. A SEP does not have the start-up and operating costs of a conventional retirement plan and allows for a contribution of up to 25 percent of each employee's pay.

You can invest in a wide range of financial products in your IRA such as stocks, bonds, mutual funds, ETFs, Annuities, CDs, REITs to highlight the most popular. ***You must consult with your accountant or tax professional*** to determine which IRA account is most beneficial to you.

401K Accounts:
401(k) Plan is a **defined** contribution plan where an employee can make contributions from his or her paycheck either before or after-tax, depending on the options offered in the plan. The contributions go into a **401(k)** account, with the employee often choosing

the investments based on options provided under the plan.

Margin Accounts:
A **margin account** is a brokerage **account** in which the broker lends the customer cash to purchase securities. The loan in the **account** is collateralized by the securities and cash. Be aware: Margin accounts can involve more risk than is prudent for many investors. I do not use Margin accounts in my practice. I truly believe this is a sophisticated tool for only the most experienced and disciplined investors.

Corporate Account:
A brokerage account used by corporations that wish to invest in securities and interest-bearing instruments.

Revocable Trust:
Trust accounts are designed by attorneys and CPAs to facilitate estate planning, charitable giving, and legacy family planning. A revocable trust is a trust whereby provisions can be altered or canceled dependent on the grantor. During the life of the trust, income earned is distributed to the grantor, and only after death does property transfer to the beneficiaries. This type of agreement provides flexibility and income to the living grantor; he or she can adjust the provisions of the trust and earn income, all the while knowing that the estate will be transferred upon death.

Irrevocable Trust:
An irrevocable trust can't be modified or terminated without the beneficiary's permission. The grantor, having transferred assets into the trust, effectively removes all his rights of ownership to the assets and the trust.

Some of the ways trusts might benefit you include:[8]

- Protecting and preserving your assets.
- Customizing and controlling how your wealth is distributed.
- Minimizing federal or state taxes.
- Addressing family dynamics; for example, divorce or blended families.
- Helping a parent or other relative manage their financial affairs.
- Providing for the welfare of an adult disabled child

Here are five benefits of adding a trust to your estate planning portfolio.[9]

- Trusts avoid the probate process. ...
- Trusts may provide tax benefits. ...
- Trusts offer specific parameters for the use of your assets. ...

[8] Source: https://bit.ly/41MXaBc

- Revocable trusts can help during illness or disability – not just death. ...
- Trusts allow for flexibility

529 Accounts: There are two types of 529 plans, prepaid plans and savings plans.

- <u>Prepaid Plans</u>

    - Prepaid plans allow one to purchase tuition credits at today's rates to be used in the future. Therefore, performance is based upon tuition inflation.
    - Prepaid plans may be administered by states or higher education institutions.
    - Currently, 10 states provide a prepaid tuition plan that is accepting new applicants. Those states include Florida, Illinois, Maryland, Massachusetts, Michigan, Nevada, Pennsylvania, Texas, Virginia, and Washington.

- <u>Savings Plans</u>

    - Savings plans are different in that all growth is based upon market performance of the underlying investments, which typically consist of mutual funds.
    - Most 529 savings plans offer a variety of age-based asset allocation options where the underlying investments become more

conservative as the beneficiary gets closer to college age.

- Savings plans may be administered by states only.
- Although states administer savings plans, record-keeping and administrative services for many savings plans are usually delegated to a mutual fund company or other financial services company.

Key Learning Points:

1. There are a variety of different account types that serve different purposes.

2. Due diligence is recommended in selecting the account/s that serve you best.

Chapter exercises:

1. **Review your current account types.**
2. **Determine if you are maximizing the account types available.**
3. **Make sure all your beneficiary information is up to date.**

Chapter 9 The Value of an Advisor

I am often asked whether it is worth the cost to hire a financial advisor. After all, they charge you money to make you money. People say they can listen to the news to find out where and how to invest, so, "Wouldn't I be better off just keeping that fee for myself?" If only it were that simple

That is not to say that you can't do all your financial planning and investing on your own successfully. You can, if you can make the time to educate yourself, develop your resources and manage the day to day of your portfolio and plan.

There are several factors involved in deciding to work with a financial advisor and pay for that advice. To keep this conversation at 100% integrity I will address both arguments:

To pay or Not to Pay- That is the Question.

Let's start with a simple formula.

Value of an Advisor = A + E+ PLP +PD + T + M + R

A – Annual Rebalancing
E – Emotional Discipline
PLP –Personal Lifetime Pension

PD – Plan design
T – Tax awareness and efficiency
M – Day to day management
R -- Resources

If you are confident with your skill sets and performance, then have at it. Truth to tell, there are non-professionals who do an excellent job managing their investments. If you have a plan and the discipline, you do not need to pay for financial advice.

Let's focus on the simple equation of how you determine the value you receive from an advisor.

<u>Annual Rebalancing:</u>
The constant portfolio monitoring that restores asset classes to their target allocations by selling assets that have appreciated and adding to those that have declined — is at its core a risk-minimizing strategy. While it is not designed to increase returns primarily, it has, in effect done just that. Let's take a simple example:

You are most likely to hit your long-term goals with a 60% stock, 40% bonds allocation. We will use $1,000,000 to illustrate and use the actual returns from 2008 to illustrate.

The 60/40 blend finished with a value of $784,560.00 vs. the 80/20 finished at $704,380, $80,180 less! I will add that after two years the 60/40 blend grew to $915,735.00 while the 80/20 blend only reached $872,442! While you may have started your portfolio at 60/40 people are very reluctant to rebalance when stocks are rising. Human nature. But as you can see, rebalancing would have cost you less loss and more importantly shortened the amount of time it would take to recoup your losses.

Emotional Discipline:

In chapter two we discussed the emotional reaction to stock market corrections and crashes. If you have a long-term plan to build wealth it has to include how to go through market corrections and Black Swan events, in my professional opinion. In my career I have seen it to be true that those who stay the course, take advantage of the buying opportunities win. They come out ahead every time. Why? Because people tend to Sell low and Buy high, which is a recipe to lose money. Having a seasoned advisor who will keep you focused on your plan, provide you with calm, reflective advice is worth its weight in gold! According to Russell Investments, the cost of "emotional behavior" for the average stock fund investor cost them 2% annually from 1984-2016. Hard numbers, The Russell 3000 Index grew 10.7% average annual return versus the "average investor" only 8.7%!

Plan Design:

A competent Financial Advisor will have access to planning tools and intellectual capital that is not readily available to the general public. In addition, we have access to a massive amount of historical reference for guidance in addition to proprietary institutional modeling that can add tremendous value. Equally important is the advisor's skill and experience in coordinating various asset classes, tax and estate planning resources and the ability to lead a team effort between your CPA, attorney and other financial professionals.

<u>Tax Awareness:</u>

Taxes are a drag! Just like flying an airplane, drag slows you down. It makes it harder to rise higher! According to Russell Investments, the average tax drag on large cap stocks for the five years ending June 2018 was 1.79% per year. The slide below shows a ten-year hypothetical of tax drag.

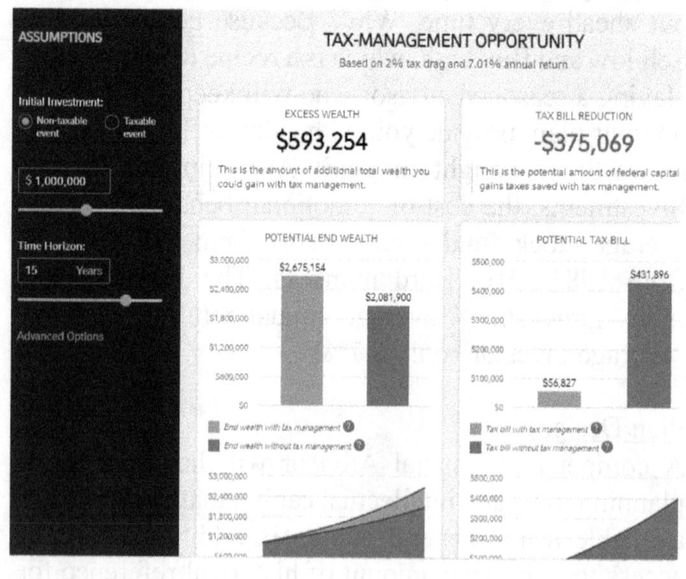

Every time I use this tool, I ask:

"What would an extra $593,000 do for you? How does that affect your emotional state, your family and how does that make you feel? "

The bottom line: if you can potentially keep more of your profits, Do It!

Day to Day Management:

There are so many details that come to mind about day-to-day management and a financial advisor will focus of the most common.

1. Dividend and interest collection
2. Maturing assets
3. Securities Reorganization (stock splits, corporate activity such as mergers, rights offerings, corporate spin-offs, to name a few)
4. Portfolio analysis and allocation adjustments
5. Capital markets research
6. Distributions and remittances
7. Documentation
8. Custodial services

Resources:
Every one of us has extensive resources in our field of work and other endeavors we pursue actively. We, in the financial services space have:

- Direct access to large, diverse research departments.
- Direct access to global money managers and asset managers
- Direct access to specialized professionals in areas such as 401Ks, pension planning, insurance, investment banking, to name a few.
- Relationships across the industry.

This would a good time to discuss how advisors get paid. Primarily there are two different platforms.

1. Commission based: you pay per transaction.

2. Fee based: The account is charged a fee; typically, a percentage of the account total.

There are many reasons an investor may choose paying commissions versus paying a fee for management. For commissions it may be advantageous for a self-directed account who may only make a few transactions annually. On the other hand, accounts that employ professional money management connected to a comprehensive financial plan may find paying an annual fee more cost effective. As well, the advisor's income is directly aligned with the client's growth goals eliminating any conflict of interest.

Key Learning Points:

- Financial advisors can bring an abundance of valuable resources and expertise to the table.
- Hiring a competent financial advisor can free up valuable time for you.

Chapter Exercises:

- Reflect on the value-added deliverables you are currently receiving from your financial advisor.
- If needed, request more services from your advisor.

Chapter 10 – Trading versus Investing. The Key Differences

Folks, this would be a good place to have a conversation about the difference between trading and investing. Here are some key concepts:

1. Each approach requires a vastly different set of skills, resources, and time management.

2. It is a personal choice. Do your homework and understand what you are getting into.

3. They are not mutually exclusive.

Trading:
A strategy that seeks to profit from rapid price changes. It is traditionally a short-term approach with trades that can last for a few minutes to as along as a few weeks. You will need volatility. It can and may entail rapid loss of your money. It can and may produce high rates of profits. You should be aware of the rules of taxation for trading. Please consult your tax professional. Traders need to devote considerably more time to this strategy than other investment approaches. You should have a strong skill set in chart reading. You should have a clearly defined SELL discipline--to limit loss and harvest gains.

Investing:
A strategy to profit from the growth of a company long term, typically 3 years or longer. It is a strategy to participate and share in the multi-year growth of companies and the global economy. Long term investors may also benefit from innovation and new technologies. You are matching long term goals with growth & income potential over long periods of time. As an example:

$10,000 invested into the S&P 500 in 1980 through July 2022 grew to $1,003,074.96![10]

That growth is an 11.38% average annual return![11]

Whether you want to trade your account or invest for the long term educate yourself. There are numerous books you can read and gain useful information. Also, discuss the benefits and pitfalls of each strategy with your advisor.

Any conversation about investing in the liquid financial markets would be incomplete without a

---

[10] Source: https://www.officialdata.org/us/stocks/s-p-500/1980?amount=10000&endYear=2022

[11] Source: https://www.officialdata.org/us/stocks/s-p-500/1980#:~:text=Stock%20market%20returns%20since%201980,%2C%20or%2011.38%25%20per%20year.

discussion on selling an investment. There are many reasons to sell:

- Lack of performance
- Taking profits. (Always the hoped-for reason)
- Sector rotation (the movement of money invested in stocks from one industry to another as investors and traders anticipate the next stage of the economic cycle.)
- Loss Limit.

It is loss limit I would like to discuss with you. Limiting financial loss is a widely known concept in business. One of the biggest advantages of investing in publicly traded securities is liquidity. If the reasons you invested in a particular security are no longer valid, if company fundamentals have turned negative and your investment has lost money, you can "limit" further loss by selling. This liquidity allows you to reinvest your money where you think you have growth and/or income potential.

Like anything else in money management, you need to have a working strategy that fits your comprehensive financial plan. With a skilled advisor you can develop a Loss Limit plan that is best for you.

Let's talk about the difference between a "fad" and a "trend. First let's look at the definition of both.

A *fad* is an intense and widely shared enthusiasm for something, especially one that is short-lived and without basis in the object's qualities, a craze.[12]

A *trend* is a general direction in which something is developing or changing.[13]

On Wall Street, there is an old saying:

The trend is your friend

While I know of no saying about fads on Wall Street, I will take license and give you one of my own.

Fads are bad. When they are gone, you go with it.

Let's look at some famous fads vs trends.

The Tulip Fad: We discussed this earlier in Chapter 2. Everyone thought tulips were the greatest thing in the world. I cannot explain nor do I understand why people placed any monetary value on tulips. Yes, they are beautiful. But value as an asset? I don't get it. And with full disclosure, I wasn't there so I can only wonder what people were thinking.

---

[12] Source: https://www.google.com/search?q=definition+of+a+fad&oq=definition+of+a+fad&aqs=chrome...69i57j0i512l2j0i22i30l3j0i10i22i30j0i15i22i30l3.4344j1j15&sourceid=chrome&ie=UTF-8

[13] https://bit.ly/definitionofatrend

Two other fads that come to mind are Game Stop and crypto-currency.

GameStop, a money-losing video- and computer-game retailer with 5,000 brick and mortar stores facing a bleak future as game-buying shifted from physical products to digital downloads, seemingly had nowhere to go but down. Short sellers had piled into its stock, betting that it was on a glide path to extinction.

Suddenly, in January 2021, the shares took off. On the first trading day of that year, they opened at \$4.33 per share and closed at \$17.25. On Jan. 29, they closed at **\$325,** a day after hitting an intraday peak of **\$483**. As of this writing the stock has been trading in a range of \$90 to \$100 per share.[14]

What caused this fad? As it turned out chat room investors like Robin Hood decided to put the squeeze to short sellers. This was the "little guy" sticking it to the man! Amateur investors got caught up in the craze, some who bought on margin, and many were decimated with the wild swings. Imagine if you were one of the investors who bought at \$325? Your losses are almost 70%. OUCH!! Hard lessons learned for many.

Crypto currency. This is a new phenomenon. It is too soon to know whether or not this will be a fad or a trend. Time will tell. That being said, I offer a word of caution. Like every high-risk investment, you need to apply prudent thinking and not allow "greed" to drive

[14] 12/13/2022

your judgement. As a personal rule I invest less in high-risk items for two reasons.

1. It is my form of risk management. If I lose my entire investment, it does not change my life.

2. If my analysis is correct, I may stand to make an enormous gain on my investment.

Let's look at the chart below as an example. The stock is Meta Platforms, formerly known as Facebook. When Facebook was founded in 2004 who knew how it would turn out? It was a whole new paradigm. Was it a fad or a trend? As you can see in the circled area of the chart not long after coming public the stock tanked. It plunged from $38.23 to $18.06. Big OUCH! Maybe some folks surmised Facebook was a flash-in-the-pan fad and sold. Selling begets selling. Also consider that a large percentage of the stock was traded prior to the general public having access to it. Many of those investors may have pulled out in order to take a fast profit.

It took another 19 months before the stock recovered to 38.23. The world bought into the social media trend and now social media is a dominant force in our lives. Facebook stock price took off like a rocket to the Moon! It hit an all-time high of $378.69! Breathtaking!

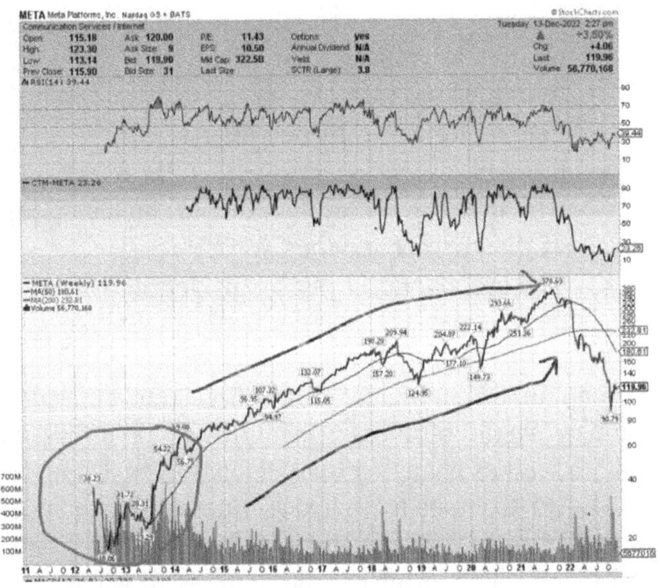

Trends are usually triggered by supply & demand imbalances or technology breakthroughs and innovation. Look at the list of technological advances in the business environment just since1980.[15]

<u>The 1980s to the 2020s</u>

- Fax machines give way to scanning and email/texting.
- Answering machines have evolved into AI enhanced voicemail on multiple devices.

[15] https://www.efax.com/blog/tech-of-the-1980s-and-today

- Floppy disks essentially replaced by direct online downloads, zip files, the Cloud and thumb drives.
- Pagers. Replaced by cell phones.
- Cassette tapes gave way to CDs and DVDs which are now used less due to the bandwidth of the internet and the Cloud.
- The cell phone: it just keeps getting more and more capable.

A trend in technological innovation kept emerging. The way we did business was improving on a massive scale as well as changing our personal lives. Using the NASDAQ Composite Index as reference, the index moved from 619.02 in January 1980 to 11,147 as of 12/14/2022. That is an 18-fold increase in value. That is fun—not to mention fertile ground for investors!

AT&T, Xerox, Hewlett Packard, IBM, & General Electric.

AT&T was listed on the New York Stock Exchange on September 4th, 1901! The telecom sector was still in its infancy with 356,000 telephones in America. Currently the number of people that own a smart and feature phone is 7.26 billion, making up 90.72% of the world's population. [16] WOW!

While AT&T is still a global telecom leader companies like Apple have also emerged, creating massive

---

[16] (Source: https://www.bankmycell.com/blog/how-many-phones-are-in-the-world)

amounts of new wealth while making life better. To demonstrate how trends change let's look at the math. $10,000 invested in Apple stock in 2012 is worth $106,000![17] Yet AT&T stock lost 19% of value. Remember with innovation comes the change in leadership.

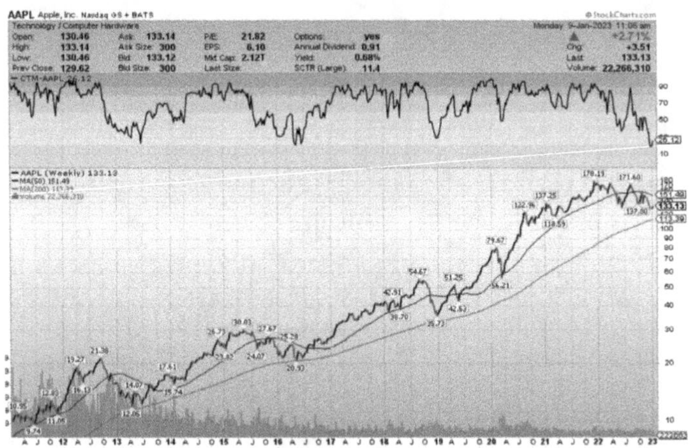

[17] https://www.fool.com/investing/2022/06/22/if-invested-10000-apple-2012-how-much-today/

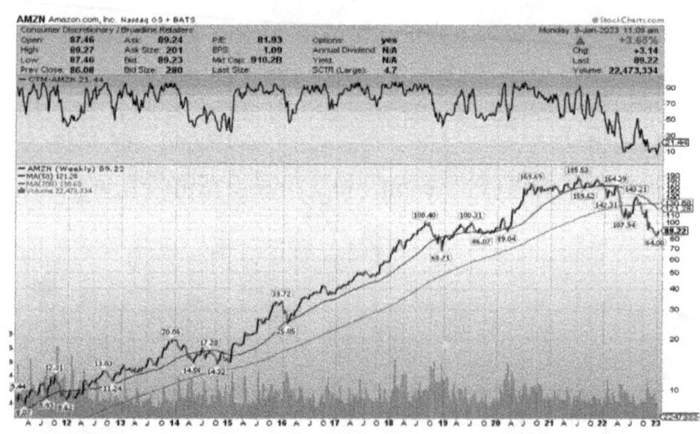
AMZN Amazon.com, Inc. Nasdaq GS + BATS
@StockCharts.com
Consumer Discretionary / Broadline Retailers
Monday 9-Jan-2023 11:09 am
Open 87.46
High 89.27
Low 87.46
Prev Close 86.08
Ask 89.24
Ask Size 201
Bid 89.23
Bid Size 280
P/E 81.93
EPS 1.09
Mkt Cap 910.2B
Last Size
Options yes
Annual Dividend N/A
Yield N/A
SCTR (Large) 4.7
Chg +3.14
Last 89.22
Volume 22,473,334
AMZN (Weekly) 89.22
A J O 12 A J O 13 A J O 14 A J O 15 A J O 16 A J O 17 A J O 18 A J O 19 A J O 20 A J O 21 A J O 22 A J O 23

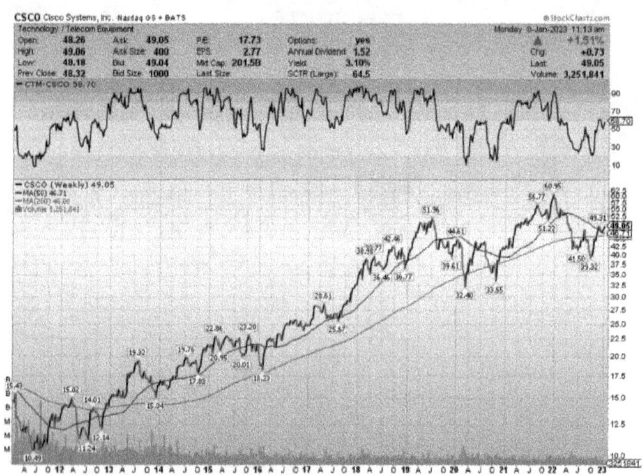
CSCO Cisco Systems, Inc. Nasdaq GS + BATS
@StockCharts.com
Technology / Telecom Equipment
Monday 9-Jan-2023 11:13 am
Open 48.26
High 49.06
Low 48.18
Prev Close 48.32
Ask 49.05
Ask Size 400
Bid 49.04
Bid Size 1000
P/E 17.73
EPS 2.77
Mkt Cap 201.5B
Last Size
Options yes
Annual Dividend 1.52
Yield 3.10%
SCTR (Large) 64.5
+1.51%
Chg +0.73
Last 49.05
Volume 3,251,841
CTM-CSCO 58.70
CSCO (Weekly) 49.05
MA(50) 46.71
A J O 12 A J O 13 A J O 14 A J O 15 A J O 16 A J O 17 A J O 18 A J O 19 A J O 20 A J O 21 A J O 22 A J O 23

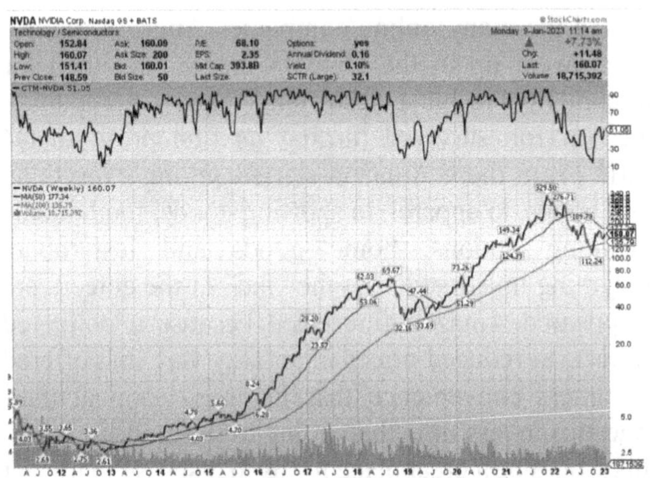

APPL, AMZN, CSCO, NVDA

So, it begs the question,

How do you know if some new idea is a fad or trend?

There is no algorithm or formula I know of to generate that answer. From my experience you need to wait and see if the initial excitement passes or does this new idea, innovation, etc change the world? Is demand for this new product growing? Will this become the new paradigm?

Let's use Amazon as an example. In 1995 Amazon sold its first book online. By 1998 the company issued

stock. Like many online companies Amazon seemed to be swept up in the Dotcom craze. And then the Dotcom bubble burst destroying many e-companies. But Amazon survived turning its first profit in Q4 2001! From there Amazon started selling everything from books, to apparel, to sporting goods, food, media streaming options, home goods and just about everything imaginable. As the "fad" of the dotcom era disappeared Amazon flourished because it delivered products at reduced prices in an easy way that offered consumers convenience that let them shop at their fingertips in less time than going to the mall.[18]
This would be a great place for us to discuss the impact of that evolving technology. As we referenced above how technology has changed how we work let's see how it changed our lives and society in general.

In 1844, Samuel Morse sent the first telegraph. Revolutionary! Communication went from weeks to mere minutes. By 1866 a trans-Atlantic cable had been laid allowing rapid communication between Europe and North America. Commercial activity reached a pace never thought possible.

The next evolution of communication came in 1876 with the invention of the telephone. Information could be shared instantly. Someone in New York could

---

18 https://en.wikipedia.org/wiki/History_of_Amazon#:~:text=Amazon%20was%20founded%20in%20the,with%20World%20Wide%20Web%20access.

transact business with someone in California at will. The world was becoming smaller.

If we fast forward to the late 20th century computers changed every aspect of our lives from doing business, research, communication, medical applications and treatments, to entertainment via streaming services, to name a few. I remember in 1995 we were just starting to use intra-office email. Now the world revolves around emails. More business is done online now than ever before and this trend is still growing.

And for everyday investors, like you and I, the opportunities are astounding. We have gone from Bell Telephone to General Electric founded by Thomas Edison in 1892, to Ford, GM, Chrysler, to IBM, to Hewlett Packard, to Apple, Microsoft, to Google to Amazon to name of few. Untold trillions of dollars of wealth have been created. And since we humans love innovating, I suspect many more opportunities are just on the horizon.

A byproduct of all this innovation is globalism. The world is connected. Business is done easily and quickly whether you are in America, Europe, or Asia. The upside is obvious, but the downside is that if growth in Europe slows it may very likely affect profits and commerce in the rest of the world. Changes in currency valuations can either increase or decrease sales from one country to another. Global outlook is now part of the recipe and must be baked into your long-term plan.

Key Learning Points:

- There are significant differences between trading versus investing. Risk versus reward, expenses and taxation.
- Determine which strategy or a blended approach is best for you.

Chapter 11 – Everyone is Unique! What type of investor are you?

If there is anything I have witnessed in my career it is that everyone's needs, wants and desires are unique to each of us. And especially when it comes to money we need to pay for our lifestyle and living expenses after you stop working at your job. The needs of a woman or man in their early 30s are vastly different from a woman or man in their late 50s or in their 70s. So, let's look at some of the basic challenges and goals of several types of client situations we work with.

"What type of investor you are will change and evolve as your life does"

What type of investor are you is a question each of us must answer. And it is not a "one time" thing. What type of investor you are will change and evolve as your life does. First let's look at age/experience. Then we will discuss life events that dictate/lead your investment approach.

Young people:
Mid 20s to mid-30s. Just arrived to the party. They are building their careers, acquiring skill sets and experience to keep moving forward. These folks are in the early stages of their careers and are just starting to save and invest. They need to create their "money

team." CPA, attorney, financial advisor etc. Time is on their side to a degree.

Here is the synopsis:

1. First and foremost, they need to learn about the markets They need to learn the differences among stocks, bonds, mutual funds, ETFs et al, and a hard-core lesson in Risk Management. (There I go again, focusing on managing downside to lose as little as reasonably possible) 😊

2. I would stress the long-term growth potential of *investing* versus trading and timing markets. Set up automatic savings and contributions to investment accounts.

3. Get your vision and then build your financial plan to achieve your vision. This is a very powerful exercise and I have seen it change lives.

    - What is it that you want out of life?
    - Do you want build companies?
    - Do you want to give back to society?
    - Do you want to travel the world?
    - When do you want to achieve financial independence?

These are some of the questions to ask yourself to develop your vision.

4. With the benefit of time on their side they can add more aggressive (and riskier) investments to their long-term planning.

5. They tend to be "fad driven" to the exclusion of creating a more balanced allocation model. In English, I vividly remember a lot of young people completely sold on the Dotcom stocks. They were all going to "the promised" land of investing. Making fat double digit returns was a "given"! And then….KABOOM! ***This validates the old axiom: Never put all your eggs in one basket.***

6. Automate contributions to savings accounts, retirement plans and investment accounts. I encourage you to do this monthly.

I. Halfway there: 36- 50 years old. They are carrying more financial responsibility with the responsibilities of a home, family and a career, and are in their peak earnings years. Now is the time to make all the accounts produce. They need:

   - Effective risk management. Whatever big economic selloffs are ahead they need to lose less. In other words, they need to exert more caution and adjust their downside risk.

- It's time to begin using tools to build lifetime incomes for their retirement.

- Begin exploring legacy and estate planning resources.

- Health care planning becomes critical as they begin to age.

II. Lock it Down: 51-65: Retirement or "chapter 2" of their lives is just over the next hill. It is on your horizon, and you can see it. Now is the time to put in place the tools and solutions that will pay you income for life and preserve your legacy. These folks need to:

- Review their beneficiary designations. You want your legacy distributed according to your wishes. Like your will you should review your beneficiary designations every few years

- Complete any remaining estate planning such as a living will, health care proxies, powers of attorney, transfer of assets to trusts, to name a few. You never want to be in a position to have make decisions when you are unprepared and highly emotional. Getting these matters in order will save you and your loved ones pain and agony.

- Make sure you have a capable executor or executrix and backups—either alternates or successors. What happens if your executor/executrix is no longer capable of performing these duties? What happens if they die? What is they simply no longer want the responsibility? Having secondary and tertiary candidates will keep continuity in your plan and avoid agonizing delays in distributing your estate.

- Utilize Income for Life strategies that let you live the way you want to. About 40 percent of all U.S. households where the head of the household is between 35 and 64 are expected to run short of money in retirement, according to a 2019 report by the Employee Benefit Research Institute. This is preventable with proper planning.

- Implement enhanced Risk Management guidelines for your investments. You no longer have 30 years to grow your money. Consider having a "sell price" when investments are losing you money. Have a strategy to manage profits. Be aware of economic policy changes. As an example, when monetary policy changes, i.e: interest go up, what does that mean to your growth stock? To your bond portfolio?

- Implement health care insurance solutions. According to the 2022 Fidelity Retiree

Health Care Cost Estimate, the average retired couple at age 65 can expect to spend around **$315,000** on health care expenses in retirement.

- Plan your social security strategy. When you begin taking benefits will affect the amount you will receive. There are three options:

  1. Early benefits,
  2. Full Retirement Age
  3. Delayed distribution.

  You need to carefully examine your benefit options as well as any possible taxation you may incur if you work part time.

III. Divorcees and Death of a spouse: This is a special group of people. First and foremost, they are in pain. They have experienced loss. In some cases, this will be the first time they are overseeing their investments and money. They need:

- Patience and understanding.
- They may need education.
- They need the counsel of their team members, CPA, lawyer, insurance agent, and financial advisor.
- They need a plan to support their life.

IV. Mature investors playing catch-up: These folks feel they have limited time to "get it done." They can be highly emotional, which as we discussed earlier, can lead to really bad decisions. What they need most is a:

- Take a deep breath!
- A plan. A detailed point A to point Z plan.
- Support for the anxious moments. Playing catch up typically involves urgent emotions; many are feeling: "I've got to get caught up. I must get this done." Believe me, this mind set does not play well with investing. As I have stressed many times in this book: Leave Your Emotions Out of It!
- Realistic expectations
- Growth and income solutions

V. Beneficiary Payout and Inheritance

- Take a breath! Large influxes of money into your account are a big deal. A windfall that can be life changing. Slow down and follow the process.
- Re-examine your current plan to come up with integration solutions. Determine how this new money can be efficiently invested with your current accounts for the long term.

- Make sure you consult with your tax professional and your attorney.
- Review and update your beneficiaries to correspond to your updated plan.
- Recognize the amazing gift this is and the "legacy" responsibility.

VI. About to retire from your company:

Now comes the fun part. You did your 35+ years and now it is time to do what you want to. No more paycheck so your money must last. You need to:

- Consolidate all 401K accounts into your IRA.
- It is highly recommended to establish guaranteed income streams. Reliable and predictable income in retirement is a useful benefit. Please consult a registered advisor to fully explore and understand your available options.
- Get your paperwork done. Wills, beneficiaries, health care proxies, asset titling and trust paperwork.
- Design a flexible Risk Management strategy that will allow you to put risk on and take risk off as the economy changes from growth to contraction.

- Add more fixed income such as corporate bonds, CDs, municipal bonds as well as dividend paying blue chip stocks.
- Pay down debt.

Key Learning Points:

1. Know what type of investor you are and where in the lifecycle you are.
2. Be clear on your vision for your money.
3. Be flexible in adjusting your strategy as you travel the lifecycle.

Chapter Exercises:

1. Review what type of investor you are.
2. Ask yourself: Are your strategies in sync with the type of investor you are?
3. If needed, make adjustments.

Chapter 12 -- Make it Happen with 5 Easy Steps

Step 1 – Reset Your Brain

In more cases than I can remember, your view of what you are expecting from the stock market is the problem and the key reason for your results. Anything that is out of alignment will not achieve your desired result. All of us have had that "comfort food moment." When I eat a large piece of apple pie with a big scoop of vanilla ice cream, and then go to the gym to "work it off," should I really be surprised that I didn't lose weight? Of course not. When you invest, and your expectation is completely unrealistic, you simply need to adjust your expectations. For example, if you invest with a short time frame and expect above average growth you may wind up very disappointed. On the flip side, if you achieve your goal, it could be worse. Why? Because as soon as the cycle changes direction (and it will!!) you will have the same disappointment. From that two bad things will happen to you.

1. You will probably lose faith in the market and possibly swear it off.

2. You have wasted time and money.

What I recommend is you adopt this mind set:

Your investment account is a lifelong account because you want your share of the growth of the global economy. History has shown, wealth can be created this way. Again, I remind you of our $10,000 example in Chapter 2. $10,000 grew to $760,000 from 1980 to 2017!

Also, as a long-term investor you have more control over taxes and costs. To see if your expectations are jamming up achieving your goals, email me at scott.lask@wedbush.com there you can request your complimentary "Expectation Alignment Worksheet. Simply type in the word Alignment in the subject to receive this valuable tool.

Step 2 – Do Your Personal Math

You need to know the following if you want your money to be successful:

1. What growth rate do you need?

2. How much risk does your target growth rate carry?

3. What do you need in yearly dollars to live?

4. Will you need to take money out of your investment accounts to fund your retirement?

5. Do you have a disciplined, automatic savings plan set up?

Step 3 – Transfer Risk Wherever You Can

This is why insurance exists. Below is a list of risks that can currently be transferred:

- Death
- Disability
- Business Interruption
- Personal Injury
- Liability
- Auto
- Hurricane
- Flood
- Estate Taxes
- Lifetime income
- Long term care
- Health

The more of your financial position you "insure," the more stability and permanence you can add to your financial life. Let me say it a different way:

The less you're on the hook, the better!

Step 4 – Save. And then save some more!

I cannot stress enough the value of having ready cash available. Speaking from personal experience, it is not a fun feeling when you lack cash when you really need it. It is like having a hand on your throat and you cannot breathe. The stress it creates is awful and does not make for a fun night at home.

So, save. If you are already saving, increase how much you are putting away. You will never, never, ever hear yourself say:

"Darn! I have too much cash. I don't know what I am going to do"!

Step 5 – Strive to be as Tax Efficient as possible.

While I am not licensed to give tax advice nor am I a CPA, I think it is obvious to all investors that being tax efficient is smart money management. Said another way:

"Your money is better in your pocket!"

What I highly recommend, is you confer with all your financial professionals, combining the collective brain trust to design the most tax efficient plan for your money. You will keep more of your money, and you will optimize your advisory team.

Key Learning Points:

1. Get real with your expectations.
2. Do your personal math.
3. Transfer risk wherever possible
4. Save money. And then, save some more.
5. Be tax efficient.

CASE STUDY

This case study is based on an actual client however, I am using fictitious names and have used different portfolio values to insure the client's privacy.

The clients, Joe and Barbara's plan was to retire when Joe was 65 years old. They had portfolio assets of $1,500,000. Their home was fully paid, and they had no debt. To live their lifestyle, they needed annual income of $150,000. They would receive $58,000 annually from social security. (They were both high earners.) That would require annual withdrawals from their portfolio of approximately $92,000, equal to a 6% drawdown. At that rate with no portfolio growth, Joe and Barbara could theoretically deplete their portfolio in 16 years. Of course, growth would extend their assets but, what if they went through a period of back-to-back losses? As an example, what if they retired in 2008 and then went through the sell-off in 2020?

To take the pressure off their portfolio and generate their annual income need we did the following.

1. Diverted $125,000 into T-bills giving them one year's income as a rainy- day fund.

2. We re-designed their portfolio to include more dividend paying stocks and add more fixed income to cash flow into the accounts.

3. We re-directed $500,000 to a guaranteed income investment that would generate $63,400 lifetime income.

4. As a result, we lowered their annual withdrawal from their portfolio to $28,600 vs. $92,000.

For most people replacing their paycheck with their own money is a very scary prospect. The real concern/fear is running out of money!

A possible solution is to look at guaranteed income products. One of the most popular is the Variable Annuity contract. What is a Variable Annuity contract? According to Investor.gov/US Securities and Exchange Commission:

A variable annuity is a contract between you and an insurance company. It serves as an investment account that may grow on a tax-deferred basis and includes certain insurance features, such as the ability to turn your account into a stream of periodic payments. You purchase a variable annuity contract by making either a single purchase payment or a series of purchase payments.

A variable annuity offers a range of investment options. The value of your contract will vary depending on the performance of the investment options you choose. The investment options for a variable annuity are typically mutual funds that invest in stocks, bonds, money market instruments, or some combination of the three.
Each variable annuity is unique. Most include features that make them different from other insurance products and investment options. *Keep in mind that you will pay extra for the features offered by variable annuities.*

As the SEC definition says it is a contract. While I personally have found this a very efficient and effective retirement planning tool, I must stress that you do your homework. This is absolutely a long-term investment. You must be prepared to invest this money for a minimum of 8 years or longer. In my almost four decades as a financial advisor, I have found that Variable Annuities have the best probability of financial success as a bedrock investment you want to hold in perpetuity.

The modern Variable Annuity offers a wide range of investment categories and flexibility to adapt to changes in the economy and markets. Many offer

- step-up or lock up features,
- guaranteed minimum income benefits,
- annual bonuses and
- death benefit options not commonly found in traditional investments such as stocks, mutual funds, and bonds.

From a Best Interests perspective, I cannot urge you enough to have a thorough conversation with your current advisor(s). Before you make any decision to invest, know all the benefits and more importantly, know the limitations, surrender charges and schedule and taxation treatment.

Key Learning Points:

- Reset your brain
- Do your personal math
- Transfer Risk
- Save money
- Be tax efficient

Chapter Exercises:

1. Do a comparison of your current situation and plan design against the key learning points.
2. Determine if any changes need to be made and implement them.

Financial Wellness:

It seems with everything we do, every service we engage there is always a lot of paperwork and documents. Nature of the beast and when it comes to money, health planning and legacy your documents are vital/critical. Let's just reference three.

1. Wills
2. Health Care Proxy
3. Beneficiary designations.

When any one of these documents is "*defective*" your wishes may not be met.

Clearly no one wants their estate mired in litigation that divides the family or prevents key decisions from being made for the health & wellness of our loved ones.

So, I ask you, my reader, to take a few minutes to imagine what not having a healthcare proxy or an up-to-date will would impact your life? Your spouse/partner? Your children? Your parents?
Here is a list of essential documents.

- Last Will and Testament. This legal document is the foundation for successful estate planning.
- Living Will.
- Living Trust.
- Durable Power of Attorney.
- Health Care Proxy.
- Insurance contracts/policies
- Bank & Brokerage account statements
- Real Estate/Business ownership.
- Artwork, antiques, collector's items, and collections. This is an asset class.

- Professional Team contact information. (Financial advisors, lawyer, accountant, etc).

Retirement Planning Worksheets:

As the saying goes: "the devil is in the details." All retirement planning should be as detailed and thorough as humanly possible. I can say from years of experience there is a tremendous amount of information needed to create a personal retirement plan. Below is an example of some of the information you will need to assemble and analyze. For the comprehensive workbook planner go to: www.scottlask.com

Expectations & Concerns

What do you most look forward to? What worries or concerns you? Select what applies to you.

Retirement Expectations	Client	
No Work	☐	
Part-Time Work for a Few Years	☐	
Never Completely Retire	☐	
Active Lifestyle	☐	
Quiet Lifestyle	☐	
Time to Travel	☐	
Time with Friends and Family	☐	
Opportunity to Help Others	☐	
Moving to a New Home	☐	
Start a Business	☐	
Less Stress - Peace of Mind	☐	
Other:	☐	
Retirement Concerns	**Client**	**Degree High/Med/Low**
Not having a paycheck anymore	☐	
Running out of money	☐	
Suffering investment losses	☐	
Leaving money to others	☐	
Spending too much	☐	
Cost of health care or long-term care	☐	
Current or future health issues	☐	
Dying early	☐	
Living too long	☐	
Getting Alzheimer's (or other illness)	☐	
Going into a nursing home	☐	
Being bored	☐	
Too much time together	☐	
Parents needing care	☐	
Family needs financial help	☐	
Kids moving home	☐	
Care for child with special needs	☐	
Other:	☐	

Retirement Age and Living Expense

When would you like to retire? Enter your Target Retirement Age. Then, indicate how willing you are to delay retirement beyond that age, if it helps you fund your Goals. Then, indicate your living expense amount.

	Client (e.g., age 65)
At what age would you like to retire?	
How willing are you to retire later?	☐ Not at All ☐ Slightly ☐ Somewhat ☐ Very
Living Expense Amount	☐ Use My Estimate $ ________

Retirement Lifestyle Goals

Lifestyle Goals are above and beyond what you need to pay for basic expenses. Rate the importance of each Goal on a scale of 10 ⟷ 1. Needs (10, 9, 8), Wants (7, 6, 5, 4), and Wishes (3, 2, 1).

Most Common Goals		**Other Goals**		
Travel	College	Wedding	New Home	Celebration
Car	Home Improvement	Major Purchase	Start Business	Provide Care
Health Care	Gift or Donation	Leave Bequest	Private School	Other

Importance High Low 10 ⟷ 1	**Description**	**Start Year**	**Amount**	**How Often**	**How Many Times**
			$		
			$		
			$		
			$		
			$		
			$		
			$		

 4

Social Security Benefits - If available, provide your Social Security estimate from ssa.gov.

	Client
Are you eligible?	☐ Yes ☐ No ☐ Receiving Now: $ ________
Benefit amount	☐ Primary Insurance Amount (PIA) $ ________
When to start	At Full Retirement Age (per Social Security) ☐ at age ______ ☐ at retirement

Retirement Income

(Pension, part-time work, rental property, annuities, royalties, alimony)

Description	Monthly Income	Start Year	Year It Ends or No. of Years	Check if amount inflates	GPO
	$			☐	☐
	$			☐	☐
	$			☐	☐
	$			☐	☐
	$			☐	☐
	$			☐	☐
	$			☐	☐
	$			☐	☐
	$			☐	☐
	$			☐	☐
	$			☐	☐

Conclusion

I hope you have found *Let's Win – Let Wall Street Work for You!* an enjoyable read and most important, that it has helped you. My goal was to write this book in *"plain English"* and convey simple, common-sense ideas to help you achieve your investment goals. To that end, I would greatly appreciate your feedback. I ask this of you because I want to deliver to you, the very best content that can help you and is meaningful to you. So please let me know how I can do better, what else you want to learn about and issues that are important to you.

You can email me at scott.lask@wedbush.com, visit us at www.scottlask.com, call our office at 845-774-2745, reach out to me on LinkedIn or we can even do a ZOOM meeting.

One last thing. Our research has shown that the investing public needs information that they can understand, learn and digest without the pressure of being "sold." With that in mind, I established The Investors' Open Forum. This is a community dedicated to being a safe, friendly place where you can come, ask questions, learn from the community, make new friends all without feeling like you are being "sold." I know I have said that twice, but it is important. No one wants to be sold. However, we do want to buy when it will add value to our lives.

The Investors' Learning Forum meets every month, and you can view the schedule using this link. https://scottlask.com/live-events/

Thank you for reading my book and allowing me the privilege of sharing my methodology with you. I hope I have helped.

Scott M. Lask

About the Author

Scott Lask is a veteran of Wall Street with four decades of investing, money management, retirement and legacy planning experience. Having lived through—and navigated his clients through The Great Crash of 1987, the Dotcom craze, the Dotcom crash, the mortgage market collapse & Great recession to name a few, Scott has learned many of the tell-tale signs of the financial markets. He is passionate about sharing his experiences to help investors win with wealth preservation and accumulation strategies. This book is his first and represents his best efforts to codify what he has learned into a cohesive manual of sensible advice and guidance for investors at every stage of life.

When not looking after his clients' financial well-being Scott is first and foremost a devoted family man.

... *"family is everything"* ...

The best moments in my life are with family and friends sitting in my dining room enjoying delicious food and being with them!

Scott also loves playing his guitars. Having played in Rock n Roll bands Scott still has the love and the passion of playing music. He now extends his guitar playing as a tool to help teach clients and investors often overlooked investment and planning concepts. And it is fun!

Scott founded The Scott Lask Wealth Management Group LLC in 2004. One of the core values of the practice is to understand each client's relationship with money on a deep emotional level. With this insight we can more closely create a customized plan to reduce stress and worry when financial markets are volatile.

As part of his commitment to educate investors and clients, Scott hosts The Investors Learning Forum, a monthly webinar where you come to learn and share great ideas. https://scottlask.com/live-events/

Contact Us

For sales, editorial information, subsidiary rights information or a catalog, please write or phone or e-mail

Brick Tower Press
Manhanset House
Shelter Island Hts., New York 11965-0342, US
Tel: 212-427-7139
www.BrickTowerPress.com
bricktower@aol.com
www.IngramContent.com

For sales in the UK and Europe please contact our distributor,

Gazelle Book Services
White Cross Mills
Lancaster, LA1 4XS, UK
Tel: (01524) 68765 Fax: (01524) 63232
email: jacky@gazelleb

Printed in the USA
CPSIA information can be obtained
at www.ICGtesting.com
LVHW010530290124
770104LV00065B/1736